T0208290

A Journey Through Torah

An Introduction to God's Life Instructions for His Children

Michael G. Wodlinger

WestBow
PRESS®
A DIVISION OF THOMAS NELSON
& ZONDERVAN

This book is a work of non-fiction. Unless otherwise noted, the author
and the publisher make no explicit guarantees as to the accuracy of
the information contained in this book and in some cases, names
of people and places have been altered to protect their privacy.

WestBow Press books may be ordered through booksellers or by contacting:

WestBow Press
A Division of Thomas Nelson & Zondervan
1663 Liberty Drive
Bloomington, IN 47403
www.westbowpress.com
1 (866) 928-1240

Taken from the Complete Jewish Bible by David H. Stern. Copyright © 1998.
All rights reserved. Used by permission of Messianic Jewish Publishers,
6120 Day Long Lane, Clarksville, MD 21029. www.messianicjewish.net.

ISBN: 978-1-9736-6332-4 (sc)
ISBN: 978-1-9736-6331-7 (e)

Print information available on the last page.

WestBow Press rev. date: 5/22/2019

ACKNOWLEDGEMENTS

This first volume of the 5-volume set of Journey Through Torah has been three years in its preparation. The inspiration for its crafting remains still with *Adonai Elohim Tzivaot*, the Lord God of Hosts, for whom we have the utmost gratitude and Love. There have been many of our friends and colleagues involved in the reading and editing of this volume; although there are too many to include here, we extend our heart-felt thanks. Hopefully, the remaining volumes will not take as long to bring into fruition.

Baruch Hashem Adonai Yeshua, Moshichainu.
Blessed is the Name of the Lord Jesus, our Messiah.

CONTENTS

Maps of Genesis

PREFACE

Welcome to A Journey Through Torah. If you have opened the pages of this manuscript to receive an in-depth description of *Torah*[1], akin to the *Talmud*[2], with its myriad of discussions, arguments and contradictions, then you have opened the wrong book. This book is exactly as the sub-title implies – *A Journey Through Torah*. It has been designed for someone who has not fully read the first five books of Moses, known as The *Torah*. Rather, if they have read the Bible at all, they often perceive these five books as belonging to the Old Testament and, therefore, irrelevant, out-moded and of little current use. The following comments are fairly typical of most Christians and their views of Torah and its contents: "We are to keep the 10 Commandments. However, keeping the *Sabbath* (as God established it from Friday evening to Saturday evening) is also in the 10 Commandments yet isn't kept". "Christianity claims that this was "changed" by God"; "Bible believers' often view perceive "the age of the church has rendered the law inoperative"; "New Covenant Theology claims that all Old Covenant laws have been fulfilled by Christ, nailed to the Cross and are thus cancelled or abrogated", and so on.

---

[1] Torah (usually translated from the Hebrew as teaching), in this context, refers to the five Books of Moses – Genesis, Exodus, Leviticus, Numbers and Deuteronomy

[2] The Talmud (usually translated from the Hebrew as instruction) is a collection of writings from ancient times. It is composed of the Mishna, rulings of the rabbis, and the Gemara, rabbinic discussions.

Then why this book? Well, I might ask you why you are reading it now? Are you curious? Have you been challenged by a family member or friend to find something out about *Torah*? Is this a religious class assignment? Whatever the reason for your opening the pages of this book, I guarantee you will not find long, drawn-out discussions of theology, which might tax your brain cells. On the contrary, this book attempts to explain the *Torah*, the five books of Moses, in a simple yet clearly accurate way, so as you do read *Torah*, it will have deeper meaning for you. Or, at least, that is its intent.

Like every good book, assuming *Torah* is a very **good** book, which, being authored by God is a certainty, *Torah* has a preface and an introduction. Unlike other books, good or not, the preface and the introduction are part of the body of *Torah* and are essential to its understanding. So, let's begin there.

When books first began to be published, authors needed to attract their readers by providing a reason for their reading what was written. Many saw the preface as an explanation of the book's contents, a defence, if you will, for the book having been written, while others viewed the preface as an apologetic. No, not the 'I'm sorry' form of apology but the literary form, in which the author provides a personal explanation for her/his having taken paper to pen to your eye and, hopefully, heart. Since God is God, the preface of *Torah* is to be found in the first three chapters of Genesis, the first 'Book' of *Torah*. It is here the Creator of the universe describes how He created, well, the universe and, especially, the earth. As is the style in *Torah*, God's preface is the story of creation of the world and the love and care He took in its creation. This also tells us a good deal about God, His power, His vastness and His desires. Reading the preface of *Torah* is a little like reading a short love story about the Potter and His Creation. But, then, the introduction to *Torah*, provides us with a reason for reading further into the five Books. As you read further into this brief exploration of *Torah*, written just for you, you may see how we human beings have a habit of often spoiling the blessings given to us. Now the tension begins to build, as we learn why *Torah* was written. So, I urge you to sit back in a comfortable chair or sofa, have a cup of tea, coffee or water close by your side and open the first book of God's Story of His desire for a relationship with you and with me. Before we proceed, let me introduce you to *Rebbe*. Rebbe will point the way to a particularly interesting fact or a significant learning which comes through the pages of God's *Torah*. Enjoy your reading of God's Life Instructions, God's *Torah*.

Hi, folks. I am Rebbe. I will point you to interesting, points to ponder and significant learnings.

B'RESHEIT - THE BOOK OF GENESIS
INTRODUCTION

Every good story must have a good opening. Have you ever thought of the door that bars or invites you into a room? You can tell a good deal about a room or a house by its door. Some doors are dull and drab, sometimes giving a false impression of the vibrant space just beyond its threshold. Other doors are flamboyant and bright, shouting out life and energy; these doors prepare you for how you will receive the space just beyond it. And so it is with the Book of Genesis – this is the door to the Scriptures, the door to the stories that tell of the history of the Jewish people and as those who are not Jewish, also known as Gentile or *goyim*, nations, and who are coming to an understanding of their relationship to our most holy *Abba*, the Ruler of the universe and the Lover of our souls.

I know you love to learn, or you wouldn't be reading this page right now and I know you, like many other people, young and old, love to learn through stories. This has been the way of learning ever since man was created. Countless generations of children have learned through the stories told them by their parents and by their leaders, teachers and others who helped them develop an understanding of their heritage and of the culture into which they are born.

Our loving God shares His story with us in *Torah* and begins that story with *B'resheit*, in the beginning, in Hebrew and, in English, the name of the door to *Torah* is Genesis, which means many things: history of, origin, birth, generation and genealogy. Genesis, the first book of the Bible and the first book of *Torah*, is the door that leads us into the fascinating story of our Almighty God's relationship with His people. Before you go any further in your reading, though, you might want to read the first few chapters of the Book of Genesis.

How is Genesis Structured?

That's a good starting point for our look at *Torah* – how is the first book of *Torah* structured? If you have read through the entire Book of Genesis, in a traditional English Bible, you may notice it has very clear divisions, into chapters. However, in the Hebrew Bible, the original language of *Torah*, the divisions are called *Parashot*, Readings. There are 54 weekly readings, each divided into 8 sections. Each section, called *Aliyah* or the honour of being called-up to read *Torah*, as well as immigrating to Israel, is to be read daily, with the full *Parashah* read on *Shabbat*, which is *Yahweh's*[3], the Lord's Day of Rest. In this overview of Genesis, we will use both the weekly *Parashah* and chapters as our guides. The version of Scripture used in Volume 1 of *A Journey Through Torah*, *B'resheit*, Genesis, is The Complete Jewish Bible, translated by Dr. David Stern. Throughout this Volume, and indeed through the other four, you will not find the original Hebrew being used; rather, you will only find the English transliteration. Whenever an English transliterated Hebrew word is used, it will be in a different font. This has been a deliberate choice, given many, if not most, of those reading this volume will not be Jewish, although that would be delightful if you are, and probably will not have a background in the Hebrew language. So, let's continue with an outline of the major divisions of Genesis.

---

[3] There are many Names for God. Yahweh is built upon the understanding "I AM." Other names used for God in this series are 'God', 'Lord', 'HaShem' and 'Elohim'

The first part of the Book begins with the preface, as I explained earlier. This is Chapter One, verse one, to the end of Chapter Two, verse 24. Here we find two versions of the same story, the Creation Story. The debates and arguments over the reasons for two versions of this glorious story have been endless and continue unabated, as if someone actually knows the truth about this, which, of course, they don't. As you read both accounts of Creation, do you get a sense of why God, the Supreme Being, wanted the world and its inhabitants? Let's just read a little from these two stories: *Let Us make man in Our image, according to Our likeness. They will rule the fish of the sea, the birds of the sky, the livestock, all the earth, and the creatures that crawl on the earth.* (Genesis 1:26) "Let Us make man in Our image", how cool is that! Have you figured out why He had that desire? Yes, of course, He wanted a relationship with someone with whom He could communicate; He wanted to discuss, to play with, perhaps to debate and argue with in a loving way. I know, you may be thinking, how does He know that? Well, as you read in the preface to *Torah*, just a bit further, you come across these words, *God blessed them, and God said to them, "Be fruitful, multiply, fill the earth, and subdue it. Rule the fish of the sea, the birds of the sky, and every creature that crawls on the earth."* (Genesis 1:28) Do you think God merely wanted to sit back and watch His creations, as they did their thing? Well, the answer to that question is hidden within *Torah* and you will discover that for yourself, as you read on further.

The second major part of Genesis (*Parashah* 2 to *Parashah* 6) introduces the major conflict of *Torah* and, indeed, all of the Bible, the conflict between God and Sin, the mortal enemy of all humans. This battle of Good versus Evil has been with us ever since evil was spawned. We can see this scriptural battle played out even in our radio programs of days past (The Lone Ranger, the Shadow) and our television series today (Batman, Spiderman, Superman).

In Chapter Three of *Torah* we are introduced to evil who,

in the form of a walking serpent, interferes with God's plans for, *Adom*, Adam, and *Chava*, Eve. How God reacts to this interference tells us just how angry and upset He really is, judging by the consequences of the introduction of evil into *Torah*. I urge you to read this part carefully, Chapters Three and Four. Believe it or not, the rest of *Torah* and, indeed, the entire Bible deals with this conflict between good and evil, in one form or another.

The other parts of the Book of Genesis are not as short as these two. The third part of Genesis begins with Chapter Five, with a genealogy of *Adom* and *Chava's* descendants. Although this may seem irrelevant to the story, it really helps place us into a sense of time and space, as we realize just how vast this story of beginnings really is. Just imagine living to be 600 or 900 years! Let's just take a moment and discuss why genealogies do appear in Genesis.

You may have caught the fact that *Adom* and *Chava* had a third son, whose name was *Seth*. Why is this important to mention? Reading *Adom's* genealogy reveals all of *Adom* and *Chava's* descendants, with the exception of those coming through the line of *Seth*, die during the flood. They were the ones who turned to the ways of evil. However, from the line of *Seth* we find *Noach* (Noah). We'll discuss *Noach's* role in God's plans shortly. Another of *Adom* and *Chava's* descendants, *Enoch*, is important to our story of *Torah*. Genesis 5 tells us, *Enoch walked with God for three hundred years after begetting Methuselah. . . . All the days of Enoch were three hundred and sixty-five years. And Enoch walked with God; then he was no more, for God had taken him.* (Genesis 5:21-24) First, why would *Torah* mention twice that *Enoch walked with God*? Traditionally, when something needs emphasizing, because of its importance, it is repeated. What is so important about mentioning *Enoch* walked with God? Simply stated, this long-lived descendant of *Adom* and *Chava* was a righteous man, what in Hebrew is called *tzadik,* a righteous one. The sages suggest he was vulnerable, because he was righteous, and, therefore, liable to go astray and be drawn into evil practices. To prevent that from happening, *Enoch* was taken to heaven, through the Word of God.

There is a book of *Enoch*, which although it never made it into the canon of Scripture, is worthy of reading. After you have read *Torah*, the Prophets and the Writings, why not take a look at the Book of *Enoch*; regard it as filling-in some of the historical gaps.

As we read further through Genesis, we are told of the very natural consequences of *Adom* and *Chava's* sin. The story of *Noach* brings a reality check, as God sees how evil human beings have become and decides to begin over again, with the only righteous person He can find – *Noach*: *But Noach found grace in the sight of ADONAI.* (Genesis 6:8) The Flood story, beginning in Genesis 6 and extending to the end of Genesis 8, is a compelling one, don't you think? Hear how God felt about how His creation had taken advantage of their freedom of choice: *ADONAI saw that the people on earth were very wicked, that all the imaginings of their hearts were always of evil only. ADONAI regretted that he had made humankind on the earth; it grieved his heart. ADONAI said, "I will wipe out humankind, whom I have created, from the whole earth; and not only human beings, but animals, creeping things and birds in the air; for I regret that I ever made them."* (Genesis 6:5-7) And the interesting part of this is that every culture around the world has a flood legend, helping confirm the vast reach of God's works. Archeologists have even found evidence of a period of flood, covering many continents[4].

Throughout the time it took *Noach* and his sons to build the ark, using stone tools only, those around watching heckled, cajoled and mocked them. Even the building of this strange

---

[4] Evidence of the Great Flood, described in Genesis 5-7 has been uncovered by archeologist Dr. Robert Ballard, in his undersea investigation of the Black Sea, in the 1980s.

structure, in the middle one of the driest portions of the earth, did not create a curiosity to hear what God was warning *Noach* and his family, just derision.

After the flood story, we are introduced to how God dealt with the arrogance people developed through their coming together as one people. The episode with the Tower of *Babel* is a compelling story, involving human beings' desires to draw closer to Elohim, God, by building a tower to Heaven and, thereby, becoming more like Him. We'll discuss this arrogance shortly.

Now we get into the meat of Genesis, the story of the birth of the Jewish People. Here, in Chapter Eleven, we are introduced to *Avram*, the first Patriarch of God's People. Throughout the rest of Genesis, we read about his family and their adventures with God. These are fascinating stories and, in this brief explanation of the Book of Genesis, we'll only touch on the highlights. So, let's get into the story of Genesis, the Beginning.

PARASHAH 1: *B'RESHEIT* (IN THE BEGINNING) CHAPTERS 1:1–6:8

Creation;
The Fall;
Cain and Able;
Introduction to the Flood

PARASHAH 1: B'RESHEIT (IN THE BEGINNING) CHAPTERS 1:1–6:8

Creation

Although it might be tempting to call the first part of the Book of Genesis primeval history, since it shares with us the beginning of everything, in reality these first few chapters have been called "man's mission in the universe."[5] Here, in the first two chapters, we read of the creation of the universe, the world and of all life on the earth, including human beings. We learn, from Chapter One, God created the world in six days and, on the seventh day, He rested. This is how we come to have a *Sabbath*, the seventh day of rest. Did God really create the world in six days? I know, this is new and probably strange to you and I don't want to confuse you with a lot of theology or arguments that support the understanding of creation. You've read and been told the earth has been around for millions of years. Let's just say that God created the earth in a time period that we understand to be six days. One particular line from this beginning of our story is very important, for here we read, *God saw all that He had made, and it was very good.* Notice we are told 'God saw'. In English, the verb 'to see' is passive and merely

[5] Rabbi Nosson Scherman and Rabbi Meir Zlotowitz, General Editors, 2000, *The Chumash*, Menorah Publications, P. 2.

connotes the process of processing physical sight. However, in Hebrew understanding, the language in which the original manuscript was written, the verb 'to see', *ra'ah*, has a deeper meaning – to know.

What does it mean for something to be *very good*, in God's eyes? One of the most important understandings of God is: He is perfect; wouldn't you agree? Of what value or importance would there be to have a God who wasn't perfect? How could we ever look up to or even worship a god that was imperfect? Right, then, we know when our Perfect God tells us something is *very good*, we know it to be perfect. Thus, when God created the world, it was perfect. But then the inevitable occurred.

I don't know about your experiences, but from mine I have found there is nothing created by man - ideas, toys, clothing or relationships - which is perfect. There is always a flaw, somewhere, always.

Adonai Elohim, the Lord God, is Perfection

And so it was with the two people who first inhabited the world, *Adom* (Man) and *Chava* (breath of life), Adam and Eve. Oh, don't get me wrong, God created a perfect man; God created a man who was, initially, immortal; He made man to walk with Him and have a perfect relationship with Him. From this perfect man, God created a perfect woman and they walked through *Gan Eden*, the Garden of Eden, together, in perfect relationship with Adonai, God.

The Fall of Humankind

But, then, both *Adom* and *Chava* betrayed *Adonai* by allowing themselves to be seduced by the serpent, which was taken over by a tempter, possibly Satan himself. Did you read of the serpent's seductive powers? Do you hear the doubt being introduced in the words? *Did God really say, 'You can't eat from any tree in the garden'?* (Genesis 3:1) Oh, how innocent and defenceless *Chava* was, in her response to this seemingly innocuous question, *We may eat the fruit from the trees in the garden. But about the fruit of the tree in the middle of the garden, God said, 'You must not eat it or touch it, or you will die'.* (Genesis 3:2-3) *Chava* believed this to be true but listen to how the serpent challenged her assumption of God's Truth: *No! You will not die. . . In fact, God knows that when you eat it your eyes will be opened and you will be like God, knowing good and evil.* (Genesis 3:4-5) What a wily challenge the serpent gave *Chava.* Once she began to doubt God's word, that's all the serpent needed to complete his task. Here is the first instance of pride bringing people down, recorded in Scripture: *Then the woman saw that the tree was good for food and delightful to look at, and that it was desirable for obtaining wisdom.* (Genesis 3:6)

Ah, the desire to be like God; what a seduction and both *Chava* and *Adom* fell for it. Ever since, people have been saddled with their own human natures, considered to be focused on our human desires, the things of the world - ambition, desires, hungers and power.

And, so, human beings 'fell' from the perfection of God and fell from God's per-fect favour, *chen*, in Hebrew, grace. Did they die? Well, yes they did, just not right then.

The adversary, satan, is a great deceiver!

Listen to how Adonai told them of the loss of their immortality: *You will eat bread by the sweat of your brow until you return to the ground, since you were taken from it; for you are dust, and you will return to dust.* (Genesis 3:17-19) After such a horrendous consequence of their sin, you might have thought, *Adom* and *Chava* would have taught their children and grandchildren of the importance of being true and faithful to their Heavenly Father.

Cain and Abel

Adom and *Chava* had two children, when they left the Garden. The first born was called, *Qayin* or Cain, which means agriculture, and the second was called, *Havel* or Abel, which means herdsman. In Hebrew, names were given to people displaying what they did in life. Cain grew grain, while Abel raised livestock, predominately sheep and goats. Instinctively or perhaps having been taught by their parents, the two boys brought offerings to *Adonai*, in thanks for the fruits of their efforts. Abel put some thought into the offering he brought, as we read: *some of the firstborn of his flock and their fat portions.* (Genesis 4:4) However, Cain appears not to have done the same, as we read: *Cain presented some of the land's produce as an offering to the LORD.* (Genesis 4:3) Naturally, *Adonai* regarded Abel's offering more highly than He did Cain's, which angered the older brother. We get a picture of his reaction in the following words: *Cain was furious, and he looked despondent.* (Genesis 4:5) Why was Cain angry? Perhaps he felt God didn't value him as much as He valued Abel. But God saw Cain's reaction and asked him: *Why are you furious? And why do you look despondent? If you do what is right, won't you be accepted? But if you do not do what is right, sin is crouching at the door. Its desire is for you, but you must rule over it.* (Genesis 4:6-7) Here *Adonai* is teaching Cain how to relate in relationship with Him – *treat Me properly; bring Me your best produce; put some real thought into what you are offering Me. Don't allow sin to get a foot-hold within you.* I guess Cain didn't heed God's advice and he killed Abel, out of jealousy and perhaps feelings of rejection. Here is where we see human nature really beginning to move away from the ideal God wanted from His people and, not too many generations later, we find the behaviour of the human beings on earth to be the worst it could ever be.

Adom and Chava had many children; two additional sons are worth noting: *Shet* and *Lemekh*. In Chapter 4, we are given the understanding Yahweh has been on the minds of people since the beginning. It was during the lifetime of Shet that people *began to call on the name of ADONAI*. However, during the time of Lemekh, others took a different path, the path of violence. Read Lemekh's poem, as found in verses 23 and 24: *Adah and Tzilah, listen to me; wives of Lemekh, hear what I say: I killed a man for wounding me, a young man who injured me. ²⁴ If Kayin will be avenged sevenfold, then Lemekh seventy-sevenfold!*

In Genesis 5, we read of God's thoughts about the behaviour of His children, who followed the path of violence and whom it seems became the majority - *When Adonai saw that man's wickedness was widespread on the earth and that every scheme his mind thought of was nothing but evil all the time, Adonai regretted that He had made man on the earth, and He was grieved in His heart.* (Genesis 5:5,6) Then He made His decision: *I will wipe off from the face of the earth mankind, whom I created, together with the animals, creatures that crawl, and birds of the sky - for I regret that I made them.* (Genesis 5:7)

The Flood - Punishment

However, there was one man and his family that Adonai found was true to Him and did not worship idols made of wood and stone. Listen to how *Adonai* spoke to this man, named Noah: *Understand that I am bringing a flood - floodwaters on the earth to destroy every creature under heaven with the breath of life in it. Everything on earth will die. But I will establish My covenant with you, and you will enter the ark with your sons, your wife, and your sons' wives.* (Genesis 5:17-18) But not only did *Adonai* want a family who would repopulate the earth with those who loved Him and worshipped only *Adonai*, He wanted to repopulate all the animal life; so, He asked *Noach* to bring into a huge ark, which God commanded Noach to build, two of every kind of animal life that existed on the earth, at that time. Here is *Adonai's* command: *You are also to bring into the ark two of all the living creatures, male and female, to keep them alive with you. Two of everything - from the birds according to their kinds, from the livestock according to their kinds, and from the animals that crawl on the ground according to their kinds - will come to you so that you can keep them alive. Take with you every kind of food that is eaten; gather it as food for you and for them.* (Genesis 5:19-21)

Whether or not you believe this event actually happened, my friend, I ask you to examine the faith of this man and his family. Imagine yourself in his position – God has asked him, in a vision, to build a huge boat to carry not only his own family but two of every species of animals in existence in the world at that time. Examine the dimensions with me - *This is how you are to make it: The ark will be 450 feet long, 75 feet wide, and 45 feet high. You are to make a roof, finishing the sides of the ark to within 18 inches of the roof. You are to put a door in the side of the ark. Make it with lower, middle, and upper decks.* The volume of this craft would have been 1,518,750 cubic feet or 43,006 cubic meters. We're talking about one large floating menagerie, not unlike one of today's ocean cruise ships.

And, so, let's return to our story.

PARASHAH 2:
NOACH (NOAH)
CHAPTERS 6:9–11:32

The Flood – Redemption;
the Tower of *Babel*

Parashah 2:
Noach (Noah)
Chapters 6:9–11:32

The Flood - Redemption

There is no question that the time from *Adom* to *Noach* was a time of trouble, strife and rebellion against God. Truly, it could be considered a failure. After watching His children spiral down into chaotic sinful behaviour, it was time to start again. And this brings us to the story of Noach and a new chapter in the relationship between Yahweh, God, and His children.[6]

O.K., here we have *Noach*, Noah, and his family building this enormous floating zoo, with only hand tools and not very sophisticated hand tools at that. You may know they lived in the Stone Age, before iron was discovered. Thus, their tools consisted of hewn stone attached to pieces of wood. How long would it have taken them to complete this task? It is estimated, from clues given to us in the Book of Genesis about 144 years. Let's take a little break now. Imagine you and your family are working on a project, which your friends and neighbours all regard as idiotic. Would you have the courage to continue, just because you had a vision of God telling you

---

[6] Rav Yitzchok Abarbanel translated by Rav Israel Lazar, 2015,, Abarbanel - Selected Commentaries on the Torah: Bereishis - Genesis: Volume 1, Atlantic Publishers.

to do this? This is the faith *Noach* had – the complete trust in God to act on His Word to him. Do you have this much trust in anyone or anything? Do many of us have this depth of trust? We really don't know until we are tested, do we? In Hebrew, this level of trust is *emunah*, trust-in action. In other words, stepping out in trust of God, without really knowing where you are going or what you are doing. Man, I wish I had that depth of faith.

Well, they finished their construction, to the specifications God ordered, and, on the date announced by the Almighty, the heavens opened up and the rain began to pour down. For forty days and forty nights it rained; eventually, there was enough water on the earth to cover everything, even the highest mountain tops. Then the rain ceased, the clouds vanished and the sun emerged, to begin its task of evaporating the water and drying the land. How long did the ark float on the waters?

We are told the waters remained on the earth for 150 days (Genesis 7:24) and then they began to recede. During this time, every living thing on the earth perished – plants, animals and people. Only the fish in the sea survived.

Faith, in Hebrew –
amunah - means
Trust-in-Action

For all this time, *Noach*, his family and all the animals and birds in the ark were kept dry and safe from all harm. Then the ark came to rest on the top of a mountain, which many believe to be Mount Ararat, in either Turkey or Armenia. You may have read of the many expeditions sent out to locate this wonderful artifact of biblical history.

Forty days after having settled on the mountain, Noach sent out a raven, to determine where there was dry land. This bird flew over the earth but did not return. Then, *Noach* sent a dove, which could not find any land and returned to the ark. One week later, the dove was sent out again and she returned with a twig from an olive tree. *Noach* knew then that life had once more started to emerge from the ground. One week later he sent the dove out; this time she did not return and *Noach* knew it was time to leave the ark. On the twenty-seventh day of the second month, the month of *Iyar*, according to the Biblical Calendar, which corresponds to our April/May, the earth was dry.

It was at this time God told *Noach* and his family to release the animals and then He gave us His covenant or His promise to never again destroy the earth with water; we read this in Genesis 8: *I will never again curse the ground because of man, even though man's inclination is evil from his youth. And I will never again strike down every living thing as I have done.*

As long as the earth endures, seedtime and harvest, cold and heat, summer and winter, and day and night will not cease. (Genesis 8:21-22) This is the second of God's promises to or covenants with us. Whenever it rains, look into the sky. You might see a rainbow; this is the sign God gave *Noach* and us of His covenant, His promise to never again flood the entire earth. As we go through the *Torah*, we will read of other covenants (promises) that are still in force today.

The Tower of *Babel*

The next story that emerges from the pages of Genesis, my dear friend, is that of the Tower of Babel. It appears that only a few hundred years following the Flood, the people of the earth, who were from Noach and his children, lived in only one place in the world – Babel. In Hebrew, the name for this place, *bavel*, means confusion; however, in the ancient language used at the time, Akkadian, the word *Bab-ilu* means 'gates of heaven' and perhaps refers to the site current city of Babylon, in Iraq. But let's get back to the story. I do hope you read Genesis 11:1-9. We find all the peoples of the earth had one language and one vocabulary. As they came together from the east and west, they settled in the Shinar Valley, where Babylon stands today. They wanted to be a great people, known far and wide as a powerful people. To achieve this recognition, the people decided to build a tower reaching to the heavens, so they could have the same status as God.

I find it interesting; God looked down on them and found their little plan to be arrogant and presumptive. Listen to what He decided to do: *If they have begun to do this as one people all having the same language, then nothing they plan to do will be impossible for them. Come, let Us go down there and confuse their language so that they will not understand one another's speech.* (Genesis 11:6-7) And, at that point, all the different languages of the world were created, such that the people of Babel were unable to understand each other. What a simple solution to this problem; God created an obstacle to their communicating with each other and thwarted their plans to share heaven with Him. I find amongst human beings the greatest obstacle to getting along is lack of communication; the inability to get an idea across without insult or arrogance. Often, when we want to win an argument, rather than debate a point, arrogance and pride become more important than the idea itself. Have you noticed that?

There is another issue emerging from God's decision to create different languages. Please read the last verse, verse 7, again: *Come, let Us go down there and confuse their language so that they will not understand one another's speech.* I have wondered for many years now how it was all the nations of the earth, existing during the time of the Israelites, worshipped other gods, while Israel worshipped the One True God.

I believe the answer is found here, in understanding what *Adonai* meant when He said, let Us go down. Jewish scholars believe *Adonai* was speaking to the angels.

For example, *Rashi*, or *Rabbi* Shlomo Yitzchaki, the great

French Rabbi, who died in 1105, called these "God's Celestial Court."[7] However, it is my belief, totally without support, that these were the angels of God

> *All the world's religions originated at Babel*

who revolted against Him; in His wisdom, Adonai invited them to become the gods of the known nations of the world. This, in part answers the question for me of how all the known nations of the world came to worship so many different idol-gods. This is just conjecture and ought not to be taken as either biblical or theological truth.

There is another legend, which emerges from this time. *Ever*/Eber, the grandson of *Shem*, the son of Noah, refused to participate in the building of the Tower of Babel and, with his family, fled across the Euphrates River. Thus, *Ivrim*,[8] the only original language at the time, was retained and became the language of *Ever's* descendants – Hebrew.

> *The legend of Ever is according to Abu Isa, an 8ᵗʰ Century, CE a self-proclaimed Jewish prophet.*

---

[7] Midrash, Genesis Rabbah 8.3 – Midrash consists of the explanation, analysis and commentary of early rabbis. This particular reference was attributed to Rashi, Rabbi Solomon ben Isaac

[8] *Brown, Driver, Briggs, Gesenius (1952). "The NAS Old Testament Hebrew Lexicon". Oxford University Press*

PARASHAH 3: LEKH L'KHA (GET YOURSELF OUT) CHAPTERS 12:1–17:27

The Story of *Avram*;
Avram in Canaan;
The Abrahamic Covenant;
The Rescue of *Lot*;
The Birth of *Ishmael*

PARASHAH 3: *LEKH L'KHA*
(GET YOURSELF OUT)
CHAPTERS 12:1–17:27

The ancient rabbis claim the birth of *Avraham* signalled a new birth for humans – the first two millennia comprised of *Avodah Zarah*[9] or the period of idolatry and strange worship, consequent to the fall of *Adom* and *Chava*. According to the *Talmud, Avraham* was born in the year 1948 BCE,[10] ending the Era of Desolation and beginning the Era of Torah.

Parashah 3, *Lekh L'Kha*, begins the major Part Four of Genesis. Every part of the Book of Genesis has a purpose, as does this next part. In Part Four we read of the Patriarchs, *Avraham*, Abraham, *Yitzchask,* Isaac, and *Ya'akov,* Jacob, their lives and the relationships God created with them. We also read of the covenants our Heavenly Father created, in His love for our ancestors, for us and for your children after you. This part then tells the stories of God's everlasting promises to His children, the Israelites, and those who seek a relationship with Him, the Ruler of the universe. So, let's examine how these stories have been unfolded for us.

---

[9] Tractate Avodah Zarah 9a, the Babylonian Talmud.
[10] BCE – Before the Common Era, the generally accepted, non-religious term for the time of the Hebrew Scriptures. The term CE, or Common Era, generally refers to the period during and following the ministry of Adonai Yeshua, the Lord Jesus.

Michael G. Wodlinger

The Story of *Avram*

Avram, as this was the name given to him by his father *Terah,* was the eleventh generation after *Noach. Avram,* whose name means exalted father, lived with his family in the settlement known as *Haran*[11], situated in the eastern part of Turkey. Archeological excavations have uncovered the remains of a bustling commercial centre in existence some 3,000 years BCE. There is an ancient legend about *Avram* and how he found God.

Terah, Avram's father, was an idol maker, creating stone idols for the locals, who, although they had some knowledge of God from Noah's children and grandchildren, had created idols to represent God so they would have something physical to worship.

The following story may be found in the *Mishna, Midrash B'resheit.* The *Mishna* is a sacred book to the Jewish People and serves as a commentary on *Torah.*

Terach was an idol worshipper, and he also sold idols. One day he went somewhere, and left Avraham to sell in his place... A woman arrived, holding a plate of grain. She said to Avraham: "Take this and offer it before them." Avraham got up, took a stick in his hands and broke all the idols, leaving the stick in the hand of the largest one.

When his father returned, he asked: "Who did this to them?"

Avraham answered, "What have I to hide? A woman came, carrying a plate of grain. She said to me, 'Take this and offer it before them.' I offered it before them, and this one here said, 'I shall eat first.' Then that one said, 'I shall eat first.' The largest idol got up, took the stick, and shattered them!"

Terach said: "What nonsense are you telling me — are they then conscious?"

*Avraham answered, "Do your ears not hear what your lips are saying? " Terach then handed him over to Nimrod...*The legend

---

[11] See Pg. 100, Map of Abram's Journey from Ur

18

continues that Terah then sent Avram away from the family home and abandoned him in a cave, to be cared for by Nimrod, the god-king of the Assyrians.[12] The following, then, is the continuation of this legend.

Thus, Avram was deserted in the cave, and he began to lament his condition. God sent Gabriel (the angel) down to give him milk to drink, and the angel made it to flow from the little finger of Avram's right hand, and he sucked at it until he was stronger. Then he arose and walked about, and he left the cave, and went along the edge of the valley. When the sun sank, and the stars came forth, he said, "These are the gods!" But the dawn came, and the stars could be seen no longer, and then he said, "I will not pay worship to these, for they are no gods." Thereupon the sun came forth, and he spoke, "This is my god, him will I extol. " But again the sun set, and he said, "He is no god," and beholding the moon, he called her his god to whom he would pay Divine homage. Then the moon was obscured, and he cried out: "This, too, is no god! There is One who sets them all in motion."

He was still communing with himself when the angel Gabriel approached him and met him with the greeting, "Shalom, Aleichem, Peace be with thee," and Avram returned, "Aleichem Shalom, With you be peace," and asked, "Who are you?" And Gabriel answered, and said, "I am the angel Gabriel, the messenger of God," and he led Avram to a spring of water nearby, and Avram washed his face and his hands and feet, and he prayed to God, bowing down and prostrating himself. This was how *Avram* came to know God, or so the legend goes.

It was at this moment, *Adonai* sent the man away from Mesopotamia, to the land of Canaan, as we read in Genesis 12 - *The LORD said to Avram: Go out from your land, your relatives, and your father's house to the land that I will show you. I will make of you a great nation, I will bless you, I will make your name great, and you will be a blessing.* (Genesis 12: 1-2) And he went.

---

[12] Ginsberg, Louis, *Legend of the Jews*, 2006. Cosimo Publishers.

Michael G. Wodlinger

Avram possessed great faith, to leave the only place he knew, even though he was not treated well, moving everything he had to somewhere he did not know on the command of God, whom he could not see or touch. As I shared with you earlier, this is *emunah*, trust in action – the highest level of faith existing. And this was the trust our ancestor carried within him.

However, this wasn't the greatest of the covenants *Adonai* made with *Avram*. We read of these in Genesis 12, when God told *Avram*, *I will bless those who bless you, I will curse those who treat you with*

Avram was a pagan, before Yahweh spoke to him.

contempt, and all the peoples on earth will be blessed through you. (Genesis 12:3)

Before *Avram* became Jewish, while he was still a Gentile, God blessed him and announced that for all time those who supported the Jewish people and the Nation of Israel, the Jewish people, not just the State of Israel, would be blessed by the Ruler of the universe and those who treated the Jewish people and the Nation of Israel with disrespect or contempt, would be cursed by God. There is a mystery attached to this declaration by God, and I will be sharing that with you, shortly.

Then, as recorded in Genesis 15, *Adonai Tzivaot*, Lord of Hosts, declared that *Avram*, who at this time was quite old, would father a son. Avram found this astounding, since, at this time he was about 85 and his wife *Sarai*, was 75, well beyond the age of bearing children.

I tell you, when God wants to make a statement, He makes it a big one. Here are

Those who bless Israel will be blessed; those who curse Israel will be cursed.

the promises, the covenants, God made with *Avram: Look at the sky and count the stars, if you are able to count them."* Then *He said to him, "Your offspring will be that numerous.* (Genesis 15:5)

The Abrahamic Covenant

Then, as to seal the promise forever, to the end of days, God cut another covenant with *Avram.* We read this in Genesis 15, beginning with verse 7: *I am Yahweh who brought you from Ur of the Chaldeans to give you this land to possess."*

⁸But he said, "Lord GOD, how can I know that I will possess it?"

⁹He said to him, "Bring Me a three-year-old cow, a three-year-old female goat, a three-year-old ram, a turtledove, and a young pigeon."

¹⁰So he brought all these to Him, split them down the middle, and laid the pieces opposite each other, but he did not cut up the birds. ¹¹Birds of prey came down on the carcasses, but Avram drove them away. ¹²As the sun was setting, a deep sleep fell on Avram, and suddenly great terror and darkness descended on him.

¹³Then the LORD said to Avram, "Know this for certain: Your offspring will be foreigners in a land that does not belong to them; they will be enslaved and oppressed 400 years. ¹⁴However, I will judge the nation they serve, and afterward they will go out with many possessions. ¹⁵But you will go to your fathers in peace and be buried at a ripe old age. ¹⁶In the fourth generation they will return here, for the iniquity of the Amorites has not yet reached its full measure."

¹⁷When the sun had set and it was dark, a smoking fire pot and a flaming torch appeared and passed between the divided animals. ¹⁸On that day the LORD made a covenant with Avram, saying, "I give this land to your offspring, from the brook of Egypt to the Euphrates River: ¹⁹the land of the Kenites, Kenizzites, Kadmonites, ²⁰Hittites, Perizzites, Rephaim, ²¹Amorites,

Canaanites, Girgashites, and Jebusites. (Genesis 15:9-21) This was an enormous portion of land, given the God's people. Let's look at how much land this entailed.

Examine the map of the Middle East, below.[13] This is a map of the ancient Middle East, at the time of *Avram*. The trapezoid I have drawn roughly outlines the land God gave to the offspring of *Avram* and *Sarai*. You may notice this territory includes the current states of Iraq, Lebanon, Syria and Jordon. Of course, that promise has not yet been fulfilled; but a time will come. Most of God's promises to His people have already come to be, so this one will also, in His time.

It was in this covenant God made that He told *Avram* that the Israelites would be enslaved in Egypt for a period of time but would escape this oppression and return to the land. The promises made by God at this time, were unilateral, made by God alone, and irrevocable, made to last forever.

The Rescue of Lot

I failed to mention to you, that Avram had a nephew, *Lot*, who joined him in his journey from Haran to Canaan. Both *Avram* and *Lot* had many servants and relatives accompanying them, with a good amount of livestock. There were so many goats and sheep that the land could not sustain both families. *Avram* offered *Lot* first choice of the available land and so he chose the entire Jordan Valley, which included the cities of Sodom and Gomorrah, close to the Dead Sea, while Avram went further west into Canaan (see map on Pg. 101). This story may be found in Genesis 13.

Unfortunately, for *Lot*, war broke out between rival kings and, since Lot lived in the same region, he, his family and his livestock were all captured and taken to Shinar, which at that time was another name for Babylon, part of the Babylonian

---

[13] See Pg. 100, Avram's Journey from Ur

kingdom. When *Avram* heard of his nephew being taken away, he gathered together an army from his own men and, with God's leading, managed to defeat the Babylonians and set *Lot* free.

On his way back to Canaan, *Avram* stopped at Jerusalem, then known as Salem. He met the King of Salem, Melchezidek, whose name in Hebrew is *Malchi Tzedek,* Righteous King or priestly king. Theologians around the world believe this was the pre-incarnate *Adonai Yeshua*, Messiah or, if you are more familiar, Jesus. If you are looking for Scriptural proof, look no further than Hebrews 7, where the author describes the relationship between Melchezidek and *Adonai Yeshua*, the Lord Jesus. These verses in Hebrews 7 tell us Adonai Yeshua has been named to the order of Melchezidek, because He is recognized as both King and High Priest of Israel and mankind. In case you did not know, the Book of Hebrews is part of the Apostolic Scriptures or *Brit HaDashah* (New Covenant), also known as the New Testament.

The Birth of Ishmael

From reading the Book of Genesis, so far, you know *Avram* had two sons, *Ishma'el*, whose mother was Hagar, an Egyptian princess, the daughter of Pharaoh – a gift to *Sarai*, after Pharaoh almost, illegally, took her as his wife, and Isaac, whose mother was *Sarai*, in her old age. Each of these boys had a purpose. Ishmael, whose name in Hebrew means *God listens*, became the progenitor of the Arab nation; he was the father of twelve tribes. Should he have been born? This is an interesting question, since *Sarai*, when she was told by Adonai she would have a son in her old age, did not trust God to do that and thought she should speed things along and help God out. So, she told *Avram* to sleep with Hagar and sire a son, to fulfill God's promise. We do that all the time, I'm afraid. When God tells us that something is going to happen, our natural inclination is to *give God a hand*; often as not, this usually leads to trouble, as was the case with Hagar and *Sarai*. When Avram reached his 99th birthday, *Adonai* came to him and did two things. First, God changed his name to *Avraham*, meaning exalted father of many, since He clarified His promise to *Avraham* that he would be the father of so vast a people he couldn't count them in his lifetime. The 'h' was added to his name, in order to honour God, through Avraham's offsprings. Before this, the name Avraham (more often pronounced Abraham) did not exist.

The second promise God made to Avraham was he would have a son, by Sarai, within one year. She overheard the comment, as she was in a nearby tent, and laughed.

Ishma'el was the founder of the 12 original tribes of the Arab nations

However, about nine months later, Sarai gave birth to, *Yitzchak,* Isaac, whose name means 'he will laugh', because he brought much joy to Sarai. Upon Ishmael's birth, God changed Sarai's name to Sarah, which means 'princess' or a woman of high rank.

Parashah 4: Vayera (He appeared)
Chapters 18:1–22:24

The Birth of *Isaac*;
the Binding of *Isaac*

PARASHAH 4: VAYERA
(HE APPEARED)
CHAPTERS 18:1–22:24

The Birth of *Isaac*

The first portion of Parashah Vayera, He Appeared, speaks about the integrity and humility of Avraham, when he welcomed the three 'strangers', revealed to be two angels of Yahweh, God, and God Himself, believed by modern scholars to be the preincarnate Messiah. It has been three days, since Avraham's circumcision, the point at which the pain is its most severe. When Avraham saw the approaching visitors, he literally ran towards them, even though he was in such pain, showing his righteousness and his loving kindness towards strangers.[14]

From the moment of Isaac's birth, there were relational difficulties between Hagar and Sarah. It appears Hagar became proud that she gave birth to Ishmael and, when Sarah couldn't conceive, she may have scorned her. This attitude appeared to have been captured by Ishmael, as may be seen in the following observation made by Sarah: *Sarah saw the son of Hagar the Egyptian, whom Hagar had borne to Avraham, making fun of Yitzchak.* (Genesis 21:9) This so enraged Sarah, who appeared to be looking for any excuse to get rid of Hagar and Avraham's first

---

[14] Rabbi Nosson Scherman and Rabbi Meir Zlotowitz, General Editors, Op. Cit., Ps. 78-79.

son, Ishmael, she ordered him to remove both of them from the camp. At first, Avraham was reluctant to do this, as you might imagine; he believed sending the woman and her child out into the wilderness was a death sentence. However, the Angel of Adonai came to Avraham and said, *Don't be distressed because of the boy and your slave-girl. Listen to everything Sarah says to you, because it is your descendants through Yitzchak who will be counted. But I will also make a nation from the son of the slave-girl, since he is descended from you.* (Genesis 21:12-13) With this assurance, some food and a flask of water, Avraham led Hagar and Ishmael out of the camp and into God's hands. Listen to how Adonai shared with Hagar her son's destiny, *Get up, lift the boy up, and hold him tightly in your hand, because I am going to make him a great nation.* (Genesis 21:18) And, so this chapter in Avraham, Sarah and Isaac's life comes to an end. However, the adventures continue.

The Binding of Isaac (Akeidah Yitzchak)

Earlier I shared with you Avraham had great faith; he left his home with all his people and possessions and went to a place where God commanded him, without complaint or question. Now we begin a chapter in Avraham's life where both his and Isaac's faith is elevated to a higher plane. This episode is called, *Akeidah Yitzchak,* the Binding of Isaac. Adonai called Avraham to take Isaac to Mount Moriah (Genesis 22:2) and sacrifice him. Once more Avraham obeyed God. Listen to the interchange between father and son, as they travel towards their destiny: *Yitzchak spoke to Avraham his father: "My father?" He answered, "Here I am, my son." He said, "I see the fire and the wood, but where is the lamb for a burnt offering?" Avraham replied, "God will provide himself the lamb for a burnt offering, my son"; and they both went on together.* (Genesis 22:7,8) At this time Isaac was a young man; it is estimated, given the passage of time, he would be in his late teens or early twenties. He knew what was going on.

When they arrived at the site, where the Temple Mount in Jerusalem now stands, Avraham built an altar and bound Isaac on top a small pile of wood. The knife poised at its zenith, Avraham stopped, almost as if contemplating what he was doing and, in his humanity, questioning God's command. Then, as he was about to direct the knife into Yitzchak's heart, he heard a voice commanding him to stop: *Don't lay your hand on the boy! Don't do anything to him! For now I know that you are a man who fears God, because you have not withheld your son, your only son, from me.* (Genesis 22:12) Now, imagine yourself in Avraham's shoes, or sandals at the time. Many years ago, when Avraham was a younger man, in his 70s, God promised him his descendants would be so vast, they would not be able to be counted; now he has been told to kill the only one who could physically bring this about. For him there would only be two possibilities: first, Adonai would not permit Avraham to continue with sacrificing Isaac or second, once Isaac was sacrificed, God would bring him back to life. In any event, Avraham knew with perfect trust Isaac would return with him to Sarah. Listen to what he said to the servants who traveled with them to Mount Moriah, *Stay here with the donkey. I and the boy will go there, worship and return to you.* (Genesis 22:5) Well, if Isaac was not sacrificed at Mount Moriah that day, what was? And once again God provided what man needed. As Avraham lowered his knife, out of the corner of his eye, he saw movement. Let's read the account in Genesis 22: *Avraham raised his eyes and looked, and there behind him was a ram caught in the bushes by its horns. Avraham went and took the ram and offered it up as a burnt offering in place of his son.* (Genesis 22:13)

Are you able to imagine how much trust Avraham had to obey God's command to sacrifice his son? I challenge

Avraham had perfect trust in the knowledge Isaac would return with him to Sarah

you to look within yourself – do you have that much trust in anyone you know?

Do you trust God that much? I suspect the answer to the first question might be "perhaps" and I believe it might be difficult for you to say you trust God that much. Why do I believe that? Because only God can provide us with that much trust. Think about it – that amount of trust requires that we give ourselves completely over to God, <u>completely</u>. With the amount of material worth we have around us and all the conveniences available to us, why would we need to trust God? Certainly, if we had no food, no mode of transportation other than our feet or some pack animals, if we had to dig wells to provide water for ourselves and for our animals, with only stones and rocks as tools, that might be a different story. But we do not have to endure any of these hardships in the Western World. Until we do, developing trust in God will only come by our surrendering our will for His. And that requires we invite Him into our lives to begin that process of change. But now I'm getting away from the story of Torah.

Parashah 5: Hayyei-Sarah (Sarah's life) Chapters 23:1–25:18

The Wells of Philistia;
Avraham's Ethics;
A Wife for Isaac

PARASHAH 5: *HAYYEI-SARAH* (SARAH'S LIFE) CHAPTERS 23:1–25:18

From a Believer's perspective, respect for the dead and concern for the future of the living are vital components of faith in Yahweh, God. The Parashah opens with Avraham's negotiating with Ephron, a "transparently greedy"[15] member of the nation of the Hittites, for the purchase of the field of *Machpelah*, where *Avraham* buried *Sarah*.

Sarah died at the age of 127, without giving birth to another child. Avraham buried her in a cave he bought from the Canaanites, at *Kyriat-Arba*. There is another story contained in the events surrounding the burial of Sarah. When Avraham approached the sons of Het, the man who owned the property on which Avraham and Sarah lived and where she died, he was offered the grave site at Machpelah free of charge. We read of this in Genesis 23: *No, my lord, listen to me: I'm giving you the field, with its cave - I'm giving it to you. In the presence of my people I give it to you.* (Genesis 23:11) But Avraham refused: *Please be good enough to listen to me. I will pay the price of the field; accept it from me, and I will bury my dead there.* (Genesis 23:13) Why?

Well, to approach an answer to this question, I'd first like

---

[15] Rabbi Nosson Scherman and Rabbi Meir Zlotowitz, General Editors, Op. Cit., Pg. 106.

to pose a question to you. Do the people around you, who are not seeking to know God more deeply, as are you or you wouldn't be reading this book, see something different about you? When you are with people, who call themselves believers, do you see something different about them? Avraham was like that; he behaved in a different way, than did the Philistines and the Hittites around him.

The Wells of Philistia

This was shown very clearly in the incident with the wells, Avraham dug in Philistia. If you haven't read Genesis 21:25-34, please read it now. All we read in this passage is the complaint Avraham levelled against Avimelekh's servants, in that they confiscated one of the wells Avraham dug for his people and flocks, claiming it was on Avimelekh's property and, therefore, belonged to him. In fact, there were 6 wells that Avraham dug which were confiscated by Avimelekh's men.

In this dispute with the wells, Avraham operated from within a different strength – that of his God – and the standard of behaviour by which he acted was not his own but that which came from Adonai Elohim Tzivaot, Lord God of Hosts, Himself. Now this dispute over the dug wells was not just a matter of inconvenience; well-digging in those days had to be completed by hand – remember at this time, mankind was just entering the Bronze Age. Each well *Avraham* dug went through solid layers of limestone. This would have taken his men weeks to dig one well and then a small band of Philistines came and demanded the well, since it lay in Philistine territory.

Do you know what you would have done, if you had spent this

Avraham relied on the strength of YHVH (Yahweh), rather than his own strength.

amount of time doing something, then someone else, on a technicality, took that away from you?

I'm sure for most of us the temptation to fight this unfair extradition would be great. But that would not be God's way. *Avraham* was a model of meekness; he kept his strength under control. He was willing to give the Philistines the benefit of the doubt and move onto another site. He did have, at his disposal, a fairly large fighting force, recently engaged in battles to secure Lot and his family from their abduction; however, *Avraham* 'turned the other cheek' and didn't lose his temper.

Avraham's Ethics

Torah doesn't share with us how *Avraham* sought out God's direction in both the issue with the wells and the burial site for his wife and family; it doesn't have to, for we see how this man of faith relies on the standards brought forth by the Almighty, through *Torah* and how *Avraham* depends upon those. It is almost as if by adhering to God's standard of ethics, *Avraham Avinu*, Abraham our Father, has called upon our Heavenly Father to lead and guide him directly.

And it was this standard of ethic which *Avraham* took into his negotiations with *Ephron* and the sons of *Het*; he did not want to be seen taking advantage of *Ephron*. Indeed, if anything, he wanted to be seen as giving *Ephron* the advantage, as this would be the right thing to do in the sight of God. And, so, *Avraham* responded to *Ephron's* offer with: *Please be good enough to listen to me. I will pay the price of the field; accept it from me, and I will bury my dead there.* *Avraham* could not have taken *Ephron's* offer because he was a man of God; because his ethical system was driven by *Torah*. Now, again, how can I say that, when *Torah* would not be introduced for another thousand years? Scripture clearly outlines for us *Torah* is *Adonai's* Wisdom; we see this is Proverbs 8. Let's begin with verse 22: *Adonai made me as the beginning of his way, the first of his ancient works,* then we move onto verses 6 & 7: *Listen! I will say worthwhile things; when I speak, my words are right. My mouth says what is true, because my lips detest evil,* and, finally, we look to verses 12 and 13: *I attain knowledge and discretion. The fear of ADONAI is hatred of evil. I hate pride and arrogance, evil ways and duplicitous speech.* These verses speak not only of Wisdom, a creation from God's lips, but also His Life Instructions, His *Torah.* Thus, affirming what has happened, *Adonai Tzivaot* wrote His *Torah* on *Avraham's* heart, providing him with a strong ethical standard, which, for the most part, he followed throughout his life in Cana 'an.

A Wife for Isaac

As *Avraham* was approaching his old age, he felt it was time to find a wife for his son, *Isaac.* At this time in marital relations, marriages were arranged between families and *Avraham* went to extreme lengths to ensure *Isaac* married someone from his own people. And here we have an interesting dilemma; just who were *Avraham's* people? He wouldn't have approached his nephew *Lot,* since both his daughters had violated God's ethical standards and became pregnant through their father. The only other choice he had was to obtain a wife from among the Chaldeans. How was this to happen?

Given *Avraham* was too old and feeble to travel such a long distance, he sent his most trusted servant, *Eliezer,* who was of Damascus of the Chaldeans. *Eliezer* was now a Hebrew, having been circumcised and having pledged loyalty to the God of Avraham. As you read through Genesis 24, look for signs of *Eliezer's* belief. Did you notice his prayer to God, recorded in verse 12-14: *ADONAI, God of my master Avraham, please let me succeed today; and show your grace to my master Avraham. Here I am, standing by the spring, as the daughters of the townsfolk come out to draw water. I will say to one of the girls, 'Please lower your jug, so that I can drink.' If she answers,*

'Yes, drink; and I will water your camels as well,' then let her be the one you intend for your servant *Yitz'chak. This is how I will know that you have shown grace to my master.* Then, of course, *Rivka* (Rebecca) responded as *Eliezer* had prayed and he knew she was the bride for *Isaac*. Once the betrothal rituals had been accomplished, as outlined in verse 53, *Eliezer* was able to escort *Rivka* to *Isaac*. There was no elaborate marriage ritual, at this time. That would come later; for now, though, *Rivka* and *Yitzchak* settled into *Sarah's* tent and raised their family within the confines of *Abraham's* Clan.

Avraham had a good life and died at the ripe age of 175. However, before he went to be with his ancestors, he took another wife, *K'turah*, to comfort him in his old age. There is some speculation *K'turah* was, in actuality, *Hagar*[16]. Why would this be? It is quite possible *Abraham* loved *Hagar*, even though she was used to 'give God a hand' and produce a child for *Abraham*. Was *Hagar* a woman of upstanding character? Before she was sent out into the wilderness, *Torah* tells us she mocked *Sarah*, who was still barren, at this time. However, upon being 'divorced' by *Avraham* and sent away from the camp, she displayed to God her shame. Could this have been the cleansing balm that washed away her guilt?

K'turah has many meanings, according to the writings of the sages of old. Her name is related to *mekuteret*, meaning perfumed, as scented with God's commandments and good deeds, being more savoury than fine spices, and also related to *ketoret*, implying her behaviour was a fine as incense. Finally, the sages claim her name is related to *keshuah*, meaning sealed. What does this have to do with *Hagar*? The sages claim *Hagar* was chaste, after she left *Avraham's* camp, having known only *Avraham*; therefore, because of her shame, *Adonai* sent her back to remarry *Avraham*. In any event, *Yitzchak* had many step brothers and sisters through *K'turah*. Genesis 25 tells

---

[16] Midrash Rabbah on Genesis 25:1.

us, *Avraham gave everything he owned to Yitz'chak. ⁶ But to the sons of the concubines he made grants while he was still living and sent them off to the east, to the land of Kedem, away from Yitz'chak his son.* (Genesis 25:5,6) He obviously did not want *Yitzchak* and his family to be drawn away from God by *K'turah's* children.

PARASHAH 6: TOL'DOT (HISTORY)
CHAPTERS 25:19–28:9

The Birth of Esau and Ya'akov; Ya'akov deceives Esau

PARASHAH 6 TOL'DOT
(HISTORY)
CHAPTERS 25:19–28:9

The Birth of *Esau* and *Ya'akov*

The rabbis[17] claim while *Avraham's* life was characterized by *chessed*, loving kindness, *Yitzchak, Isaac's* purpose was to create a line between good and evil, represented by *Ya'akov*, Jacob, and *Esav*, Esau, requiring *gevuah*, strength. In *Tol'dot*, we discover one is not isolated from the other; strength needs loving kindness and loving kindness needs strength to function properly.

In Genesis 25, then, we are introduced to the birth of *Esav* and *Ya'akov*, the fighting twins within *Rivka's* womb. In her attempt to understand why the two would be battling each other, even before birth, *Rivka* (Rebecca) sought out God's help and was told by *Adonai*, *There are two nations in your womb. From birth they will be two rival peoples. One of these peoples will be stronger than the other, and the older will serve the younger.* (Genesis 25:23) Clearly there is a message for us today, from the two sons of *Rivka* and *Yitzchak* (Isaac) – *Esau* would be the antagonist in the ongoing battle between the sons of *Yitzchak*, while *Ya'akov* (Jacob) would prevail as the stronger. There are two levels of teaching within the story of *Esau* and *Ya'akov*, the first message being that of integrity.

---

17 Avodah Zarah 1:2,3.

Esau was the one who displayed a grave lack of integrity, as he traded his birthright for a bowl of stew. Let's revisit that moment: *One day when Ya'akov had cooked some stew, 'Esav came in from the open country, exhausted, [30] and said to Ya'akov, "Please! Let me gulp down some of that red stuff — that red stuff! I'm exhausted!" (This is why he was called 'Edom [red].) [31] Ya'akov answered, "First sell me your rights as the firstborn." [32] "Look, I'm about to die!" said 'Esav. "What use to me are my rights as the firstborn?" [33] Ya'akov said, "First, swear to me!" So he swore to him, thus selling his birthright to Ya'akov. [34] Then Ya'akov gave him bread and lentil stew; he ate and drank, got up and went on his way. Thus 'Esav showed how little he valued his birthright.* (Genesis 25:29-34) In this passage we see both parties displayed a grievous lack of integrity. I doubt very much that *Esau* was about to die, merely for missing one day's meal and, thus, giving away his birthright, given to him by *Adonai Tzivaot*, was dishonest and a denial of *Adonai's* position in his life.

By a similar token, *Ya'akov* also displayed a lack of integrity, when he took advantage of *Esau's* position and demanded his birthright in exchange for a mere bowl of stew. Why then, did God judge *Esau's* lack of integrity greater than *Ya'akov's*? Frankly, I'm not so sure He did.

Esau was a man of the field and forest; he was much more secure and comfortable being in the woods, hunting. *Ya'akov*, on the other hand, was much more a community man; he was much more comfortable being with his family, especially his mother *Rivka*/Rebecca.

The second lesson which comes through the story of Esau and *Ya'akov*, deals with whom Adonai chooses to be blessed and to

Why did Yahweh love Ya'akov more than He loved 'Esau?

receive grace. Was the fact that *Esau* was a non-religious sinner different from *Ya'akov*'s being a religious sinner?

And what do I really mean by that? Right from the beginning, *Adonai* saw which son of *Yitzchak* would love Him, in spite of their sinful natures. We see this much later, when the prophet *Malachi* wrote, in Chapter 1: *Esav was Ya'akov's brother. Yet I loved Ya'akov but hated 'Esav. I made his mountains desolate and gave his territory to desert jackals.* (*Malachi* 1:2,3) The line of *Adonai Yeshua,* The Lord Jesus, came through *Ya'akov,* not through *Esau,* who was the elder of the two boys. *Adonai* saw something in *Ya'akov,* a redemptive spirit perhaps, which he did not see either in *Esau* or in his descendants, the Edomites. We know *Ya'akov* had a heart for God, which he demonstrated many times throughout his life. However, by deceiving Esau and his father, *Yitzchak,* there were consequences to pay.

I believe *Ya'akov* needed to understand what it meant to be betrayed, as he betrayed both Esau and his father.

The line of Adonai Yeshua (The Lord Jesus) came through Ya'akov

PARASHAH 7: VAYETZE
(HE WENT OUT)
CHAPTERS 28:10 TO 32:3

Ya'akov's Lesson of Betrayal;
Leah and Rachel;
Lavan betrays Ya'akov;
the Birth of the Twelve Tribes of Israel;
a Bounty of Sheep & Goats;
Ya'akov leaves Lavan

PARASHAH 7: VAYETZE
(HE WENT OUT)
CHAPTERS 28:10 TO 32:3

Ya'akov's Lesson of Betrayal

At the urging of his wife, Rebecca, *Isaac* urged *Ya'akov*, to find a wife from his mother's family in the Chaldees. This *Laban* was the same *Laban* to whom *Avraham* sent *Eliezer* to obtain a wife for *Isaac*. This story may be read in Genesis 28. Let's just read a small portion of this passage: *Isaac summoned Jacob, blessed him, and commanded him: "Don't take a wife from the Canaanite women. ² Go at once to Paddan-aram, to the house of Bethuel, your mother's father. Marry one of the daughters of Laban, your mother's brother. ³ May God Almighty bless you and make you fruitful and multiply you so that you become an assembly of peoples. ⁴ May God give you and your offspring the blessing of Abraham so that you may possess the land where you live as a foreigner, the land God gave to Abraham." ⁵ So Isaac sent Jacob to Paddan-aram, to Laban son of Bethuel the Aramean, the brother of Rebekah, the mother of Jacob and Esau.*

It was not a coincidence, then, *Ya'akov* was betrayed by *Laban* and required to serve fourteen years for the woman he loved, rather than the agreed upon seven years.

How did *Ya'akov* display to *Adonai* his redemptive spirit? There were two instances, recorded in Genesis 28 and Genesis 32. In Genesis 28, we read of *Ya'akov* spending the night by an oasis, formally called *Luz*. While sleeping, he had a dream of angels ascending and descending a ladder, reaching from the earth to heaven. While having this dream, *Ya'akov* was aware *Adonai* was there with him and He said, *I am ADONAI, the God of Avraham your [grand]father and the God of Yitz'chak. The land on which you are lying I will give to you and to your descendants. Your descendants will be as numerous as the grains of dust on the earth. You will expand to the west and to the east, to the north and to the south. By you and your descendants all the families of the earth will be blessed. Look, I am with you. I will guard you wherever you go, and I will bring you back into this land, because I won't leave you until I have done what I have promised you.* (Genesis 28:13-15) Once again, for the third time, God made His covenant known, this time to the progenitor of the line of *David* and of *Adonai Yeshua,* the Lord Jesus. In return, *Ya'akov* placed a 'standing stone' to commemorate the moment of interacting with God Himself. Listen to *Ya'akov*'s bargain made with *Adonai, If God will be with me and will guard me on this road that I am traveling, giving me bread to eat and clothes to wear, ²¹ so that I return to my father's house in peace, then ADONAI will be my God; ²² and this stone, which I have set up as a standing-stone, will be God's house; and of everything you give me, I will faithfully return one-tenth to you.* (Genesis 28:20-23) You would think, with this promise of solidarity with God Almighty, *Ya'akov* would be a changed man. However, that was not to be the case. And once more we are privy to man's basic nature winning over. In this passage, we read of *Ya'akov* striking a unilateral, conditional bargain with God. Did *Adonai Elohim* honour that bargain? Did *Ya'akov*? Let's read on for the answers to these questions.

Ya'akov came to Haran, the land of his grandfather, *Avraham,* to select a wife from among his family. Weddings were much less complicated than they are today. First, we read of *Ya'akov* falling in love with *Rachel,* his cousin, recorded in Genesis 29, *When Ya'akov saw Rachel the daughter of Lavan*

his mother's brother, and the sheep of Lavan his mother's brother,
Ya'akov went up and rolled the stone away from the opening of
the well and watered the flock of Lavan his mother's brother. [11]
Ya'akov kissed Rachel and wept aloud. (Genesis 29:10,11) Now
the man *Lavan*, in Genesis 29, was the same *Lavan* with whom
Eliezer, *Avraham's* trusted servant, brought *Rivkah*, Rebecca,
to *Isaac*. Thus, now as a much older man, the granduncle of
Ya'akov faced him with two of his remaining unwed daughters,
Leah, the older, and *Rachel*, the younger. *Ya'akov* chose *Rachel*.
But at this point the narrative takes a decidedly interesting
turn.

Isn't it interesting *Ya'akov* stayed with *Lavan* and his family
for one month, before making known his love for *Rachel*? This
was the proper protocol of courtship, at this time. Although
Ya'akov was family, he was a stranger to all in *Lavan's* camp;
they needed time to know and to trust him. Why, then, you
might ask, didn't *Eliezer* follow the protocol, when he came to
find *Rivkah*? Were the circumstances that different?

Eliezer was not there to marry *Rivkah* but to take her to
Isaac; it wouldn't matter how long he stayed there, *Rivkah*
would not become trusting of *Isaac* any sooner. You may have
read, in Genesis 24 of *Lavan's* reluctance to let his sister leave,
Let the girl stay with us a few days, at least ten. After that, she
will go. (Genesis 24:55) Could you blame him? He was losing
one of his best camel herders. But back to *Ya'akov* and *Rachel*.

When *Ya'akov* announced to *Lavan* his love for *Rachel* and
his desire to marry her, *Lavan* agreed and a huge wedding feast
was created, *Lavan gathered all the men of the place and gave a*
banquet. (Genesis 29:22) Following the banquet, late at night,
Leah, not *Rachel*, dressed in her wedding robes, including an
opaque veil across her face, which probably only showed her
eyes, went into *Ya'akov's* tent. The practice of the day was for
the bride to enter the tent of her groom still veiled; she would
not remove her veil until after the lighted lamp was extinguished;
there would be total darkness within the tent. *Ya'akov* would

not be able to see *Leah* clearly and, quite naturally, would assume he was with *Rachel.* Imagine his surprise, when in the morning he discovered *Leah* lying beside him.

Well we don't have to imagine, listen to *Ya'akov's* understated anger, when he confronted Lavan, *What kind of thing is this that you've done to me?*

The practice of the day was for the bride to enter the tent of her groom still veiled; she would not remove her veil until after the lighted lamp was extinguished

Didn't I work for you for Rachel? Why have you deceived me? (Genesis 29:25) Why indeed did *Lavan* deceive his son-in-law? The reason given *Ya'akov* was tradition. Listen as *Lavan* explains, *In our place that isn't how it's done, to give the younger daughter before the firstborn.* (Genesis 29:26) One of the driving principles among peoples of the ancient Middle East, as it is today, is the avoidance of shame coming upon the family. If *Lavan* had allowed *Ya'akov* to marry *Rachel* instead of *Leah*, he would have brought shame upon both *Leah* and his entire family. There might have occurred traumatic consequences for this, including the killing of *Rachel, Leah* and, possibly, *Ya'akov.* However, *Lavan* offered a way to save face and to provide *Ya'akov* with what he wanted. Listen to his solution to the problem, recorded in Genesis 29, *Finish the marriage week of this one, and we'll give you the other one also in exchange for the work you will do for me during yet another seven years.*

However, there was possibly another reason why *Ya'akov* was deceived by *Lavan.* Was this perhaps the consequence for his having deceived both Esau and *Yitzchak?* Although *Adonai Elohim* used *Ya'akov* and *Rivkah's* deceptions for His purposes, there were still consequences to be paid. In *Ya'akov's* case, it appears the consequences included fourteen years of working for *Lavan*, for the woman he loved. The first seven years would have gone by relatively quickly, as we read in Genesis 29, *So Ya'akov worked seven years for Rachel, and it seemed only a few days to him, because he was so much in love with her.* (Genesis 29:20) I suspect, though, the next seven years would not have flown by so quickly.

It may be interesting to note, *Ya'akov* had four wives – *Leah* and her maid-servant *Zilpah* and *Rachel* and her maid-servant *Bilhah*. Both *Leah* and *Rachel* allowed *Ya'akov* to sleep with their maid-servants, when neither of them was able to conceive. Isn't it amazing how man often tries to 'give God a hand', when things don't go as smoothly or as quickly as we humans desire?

From these four women arose the twelve tribes of Israel, *Rueben* (see, a son), *Shimon* (hearing), *Levi* (joining), *Y'hudah* (praise), *Dan* (He judged), *Naphtali* (my wrestling), *Gad* (good fortune), *Asher* (happy), *Issachar* (hire, reward), *Zebulon* (living together) and *Yosef*/Joseph (may He add). Also born to *Leah* was *Dinah*, the only girl amongst the twelve boys. *Binyamin*/Benjamin came later and was the last boy born, before *Rachel* died in child-birth.

Once more we learn, in Genesis 30, of *Adonai*'s being with *Ya'akov*. As *Ya'akov* was preparing to leave *Lavan*'s camp and return to Canaan,

The twelve tribes of Israel came from Leah (6), Zilpah (2), Rachel (2) and Bilhah (2)

Adonai Elohim (Lord God) provided him with a bounty of sheep and goats.

Please read Genesis 30, verses 29 to 43, to see how this miracle was performed. I ask you to reflect on God's abundant blessings upon *Ya'akov*, even though he was not a fully ethical man. You might wish to read Chapter 31 and verse 13, where *Adonai Tzivaot*, Lord of Hosts, said to *Ya'akov*, *I am the God of Beit-El* (the House of God), *where you anointed a standing-stone with oil, where you vowed your vow to me. Now get up, get out of this land, and return to the land where you were born.* (Genesis 31:13) Think about God's comment about *Ya'akov's* vow and how seriously God received that vow.

With a large herd of goats, camels, donkeys and sheep, *Ya'akov* left *Lavan's* camp and headed home. Unbeknownst to him, when *Ya'akov* and his large family left *Lavan's* camp, *Rachel* took her father's family idols. Why would she do such a thing? How is it *Ya'akov* would marry someone who believed in idolatry? Do you find this strange that God would allow such a thing? What possible purpose could this serve? Perhaps *Rachel* had a change of heart and did believe in the God that *Ya'akov* believed. If that's the case, and I believe it is, then what she was doing was a noble deed, removing the idols so as to help her father turn away from idol worship. Surely, the more than 14 years *Ya'akov* had with *Rachel* in her father's camp provided a great opportunity for *Ya'akov* to witness the miracles performed by God. Indeed, *Rachel* could see the results of God's hand in the phenomenal increase of her husband's herds, whereas *Lavan's* herds began to diminish. Or another understanding might arise from the conflicts that emerged between *Ya'akov* and *Lavan*. Seeing how her father had treated her husband, *Rachel* may have decided to 'punish' her father, by removing his household gods. Pure speculation, of course.

PARASHAH 8:
VAYISHLACH (HE SENT)
CHAPTERS 32:4 TO 36:43

Ya'akov confronts Esau;
the Wrestling Match;
Ya'akov becomes Israel;
Dinah's Shame — Ya'akov's Shame;
Esau's Geneology

PARASHAH 8: VAYISHLACH
(HE SENT)
CHAPTERS 32:4 TO 36:43

Ya'akov Confronts Esau

So, now *Ya'akov* returned to Cana'an, the land of his birth, with all his wives, his children and the wealth he had amassed, through *Adonai*'s generosity. On his way, at a place he called *Machanayim*, *Ya'akov* was met by angels from *Adonai*. These were there, it seems, to protect him and all those with him. In many translations of the Hebrew Scripture, we read of *Ya'akov* sending messengers to his brother *Esau*, however, in the Hebrew Scriptures, we read the word *malachim*, angels. Thus, it seems *Ya'akov* retained the favour of Adonai Elohim, who sent angels to do his bidding. However, as we read in verse 7 of Chapter 32, the angels returned, telling *Ya'akov*, *"We went to your brother 'Esav, and he is coming to meet you; with him are four hundred men."* When faced with the prospect of seeing his brother, *Esau*, again, *Ya'akov* became fearful and once more relied on his own strength, rather than on God's, even though he knew the Almighty's messengers were there with him. As we read in Genesis 32, *He divided the people, flocks, cattle and camels with him into two camps, saying, "If 'Esav comes to the one camp and attacks it, at least the camp that is left will escape."* (Genesis 32:8,9) Then, as if an after-thought, he sought God's protection, *Please! Rescue me from my brother 'Esav! I'm afraid of him, afraid he'll come and attack me, without regard for mothers or children.* (Genesis 32:12) At this point, *Ya'akov* reminded *Adonai Tzivaot* of His promise to . . . *certainly do you good and make your descendants as numerous as the grains of sand by the sea, which are so many they can't be counted.* (Genesis 32: 13) That evening, after he sent the first camp of his servants and flocks, perhaps to take the brunt of *Esau's* anger, before he arrived, *Ya'akov* wrestled with a man, whom some theologians perceive was *Adonai Yeshua*, the Lord Jesus; however, most translations, including the Hebrew Scriptures, use the word man. Through his wrestling, *Ya'akov* was stamped as God's possession. *Adonai* put His mark on *Ya'akov*, by dislocating his hip, which was never repaired. The man walked for the rest of his natural life with a limp.

Was this perhaps *Ya'akov*'s 'thorn' or reminder that he was totally dependent upon *Adonai Elohim Tzivaot*, Lord God of Hosts, for everything? Before letting the 'man' go, *Ya'akov* demanded he be blessed.

> *Ya'akov wrestled with a man, whom some theologians perceive was Adonai Yeshua, the Lord Jesus*

In doing so, the man changed *Ya'akov*'s name to *Yisra'el*, meaning triumphant with God or 'who prevails with God'.[1] *Yisra'el* called this place *P'nei El* or the face of God, because, as he said, *I have seen God face to face, yet my life is spared.* (Genesis 32:31)

Well, as it turned out, *Ya'akov/Yisra'el* had nothing to fear from Esau; when the two brothers met, *Esav ran to meet him, hugged him, threw his arms around his neck and kissed him; and they wept.* (Genesis 33:4) All was forgiven.

Dinah's Shame — *Ya'akov's* Shame

However, that was not the end of *Ya'akov's* troubles. After he settled near the city of Shekhem, his daughter, *Dinah*, ran into trouble with the men of the city. She was taken and raped by *Shekhem*, the son of *Hamor*, the *Hivi*, who ruled this part of Cana'an. Such an action brought shame upon the house of *Ya'akov*; *Hamor* attempted to negotiate a truce between them, offering his son as husband for *Dinah* and extending a business opportunity for *Ya'akov* and his sons, as we read in Genesis 34, *My son Sh'khem's heart is set on your daughter. Please give her to him as his wife; and intermarry with us: give your daughters to us, and take our daughters for yourselves. You will live with us, and the land will be available to you -- you'll live, do business and acquire possessions here.* (Genesis 34:8-10) This was a problem for *Ya'akov*, however, because to enter into this relationship with *Hamor* would have invited idolatry into *Ya'akov's* house. He retired to think about the offer but some of his sons had other plans.

They appeared to agree to *Hamor's* offer and required he and all the males in his family become circumcised, in order for the two families to mingle. At this time, it was unseemly that the circumcised and the uncircumcised should form alliances of this kind. However, on the third day following the sons of *Hamor's* circumcision, when their pain was the greatest, *Shimon* and *Levi*, two of *Ya'akov's* sons with their male servants, stole into the city and murdered every son and male servant they found, took their flocks, their women and their children as slaves and looted their homes. And, yes, they also rescued *Dinah* from the house of *Shekhem*.

When *Ya'akov* discovered what

Shimon and Levi murdered all the males of Shekhem, following the rape of their sister, Dinah.

they had done, he was livid. He confronted *Shimon* and *Levi* with, *You have caused me trouble by making me stink in the opinion of the local inhabitants, the Kena'ani and the P'rizi. Since I don't have many people, they'll align themselves together against me and attack me; and I will be destroyed, I and my household.* (Genesis 34:30)

At this point, *Adonai Elohim* told *Ya'akov* to move his family and all their flocks to *Beit El*, the house of God. Before doing so, *Ya'akov* told his family and their servants to destroy all the idols and jewellery they had obtained from the Shekhemites and purify themselves before they began their journey. *Adonai Tzivaot* protected them along the way *While they were traveling, a terror from God fell upon the cities around them, so that none of them pursued the sons of Ya'akov.* (Genesis 35:5) You may remember, it was at *Beit El*, *Ya'akov* built an altar to *Adonai*, when he was fleeing from his brother *Esau* those many years ago, and where he had the vision of angels ascending and descending upon a ladder to and from Heaven.

When he arrived at *Beit El*, *Adonai Elohim* once more spoke to *Ya'akov*, reaffirming his name change to *Yisra'el* and reaffirming the covenant He made with his father *Yitzchak*, Isaac, and his grandfather, *Avraham*. It would be appropriate to reiterate that Covenant here, as we read it in Genesis 35, *I am El Shaddai. Be fruitful and multiply. A nation, indeed a group of nations, will come from you; kings will be descended from you. Moreover, the land which I gave to Avraham and Yitz'chak I will give to you, and I will give the land to your descendants after you.* (Genesis 35:11-13) At *Beit El*, *Adonai* told *Ya'akov* to travel further to *Efrat*, located between Bethlehem and Hebron, about 12 kilometers south of Jerusalem. On the way, *Rachel* gave birth to *Binyamin,* Benjamin, and, in the process, died. *Ya'akov* buried her in *Efrat*. If you travel to Bethlehem, you will see still today what many believe is the grave of *Rachel*.

Ya'akov finished his journey at *Mamre*, where *Yitzchak*, his father, lived and he settled. Shortly after arriving, *Yitzchak* died; *Ya'akov* and *Esau* buried him in the caves of *Machpelah*, where *Avraham* and *Sarah* were laid to rest. *Esau* then left *Ya'akov* and the brothers never met again.

As we read further into Genesis 36, we are given the genealogy of *Esau*, the founder of *Edom* and the father of the Edomites. *Edom*, in Hebrew, means 'red stuff' and refers to the red stew *Ya'akov* made, which *Esau* demanded. Eventually, *Esau* acquired the nickname *Edom*. The Edomites were ruled by 36 kings, from the time of *Esau* until they were absorbed into the Arab nations surrounding Israel. Their most prominent stronghold was *Petra*, in modern day Jordan. If you have watched Indiana Jones and the Temple of Doom, then you have seen the temple of the Edomites or *Idumea*, as they were also known, at *Petra*. Nothing was heard of them following the Jewish revolts of the 2nd Century. I find it most interesting *Adonai Elohim*, the Lord God, would devote an entire chapter of Scripture to *Esau's* people, since they eventually disappeared as a people. However, it is important to mention a few interesting facts. First, *Esau* acted generously to *Ya'akov*, even though his brother 'stole' his birthright. When their flocks of sheep and goats grew too large for the land to sustain, *Esau* volunteered to move, leaving *Ya'akov* and his family with the more bountiful vegetation. The second reason for *Esau's* genealogy mentioned in Genesis 36, is the promise *Adonai Elohim* made to *Avraham*, in Genesis 17, *I will make nations of you; kings will descend from you.* (Genesis 17:6) The emergence of the Edomite dynasty fulfills that prophecy, as *Esau* was the grandson of *Avraham*. There is a third reason for giving *Esau* so much space in *Torah* – the birth of *Amalek*. As you may know, the Amalekites played a prominent role in the History of Ancient Israel. They pestered the Israelites, as they wandered forty years through the wilderness, 'picking off' the stragglers at the edge of the camp. We read of this in Deuteronomy 25, *Remember what 'Amalek did to you on the road as you were coming out of Egypt, how he met you by the road, attacked those in the rear, those who were exhausted and straggling behind when you were tired and weary. He did not fear God. Therefore, when ADONAI your God has given you rest from all your surrounding enemies in the land ADONAI your God is giving you as your inheritance to possess, you are to blot out all memory of 'Amalek from under heaven. Don't forget!* (Deuteronomy 25:17,18)

This was the imperative which guided King Saul, when he went to war against Amalekites; unfortunately, he did not follow this and, as a result of not fulfilling

Amalek was a descendent of Esau and gave rise to the Amalekites

this demand and others, Saul lost his throne and crown, as we read in 1 Samuel 15, *Sha'ul and the people spared Agag (the King of Amalek), along with the best of the sheep and cattle, and even the second best, also the lambs, and everything that was good — they weren't inclined to destroy these things. But everything that was worthless or weak they completely destroyed . . . ADONAI has rejected you as king over Isra'el.* (1 Samuel 15:9,26)

PARASHAH 9: VAYESHEV (HE CONTINUED LIVING) CHAPTERS 37:1 TO 40:23

Yosef and Egypt;
His Brothers' Wrath;
Tamar;
Yosef in Prison;
the Prophesies

PARASHAH 9: VAYESHEV
(HE CONTINUED LIVING)
CHAPTERS 37:1 TO 40:23

Yosef (Joseph) and Egypt

Well, let's move on from *Esau* and on to the story of *Yosef*, the eleventh son of *Ya'akov* and *Rachel's* first-born son. *Yosef* (Joseph in English), whose name means 'may *Yahwey, God*, add', was *Ya'akov's* favoured son. This led to some interesting interactions between the boy and his brothers. If you have a brother or sister whom one or both of your parents favoured over the others, how might you feel? What did *Yosef* do which stimulated his brothers' hatred of him? As you read through Genesis 37, you may develop the impression *Yosef* was either incredibly naïve or arrogant. I'll leave that decision to you; however, let's read a couple of examples of his behaviour which riles his brothers.

In Genesis 37 we read, *Once when he was with the sons of Bilhah and the sons of Zilpah, his father's wives, he brought a bad report about them to their father.* (Genesis 37:2) and further on, *Yosef had a dream which he told his brothers, and that made them hate him all the more. He said to them, "Listen while I tell you about this dream of mine. We were tying up bundles of wheat in the field when suddenly my bundle got up by itself and stood upright; then your bundles came, gathered around mine and prostrated themselves before it."* (Genesis 37:5-7) Then, to show *Yosef* how much he was favoured, *Ya'akov* made him a rainbow-coloured cloak. It appears there was much blame to pass around.

Here is how *Yosef*'s brothers reacted to their father favouring him, as we read in Genesis 37, *"Yes, you will certainly be our king. You'll do a great job of bossing us around!" And they hated him still more for his dreams and for what he said.* (Genesis 37:8) and, following a second dream he shared with his brothers and parents, *"What is this dream you have had? Do you really expect me, your mother and your brothers to come and prostrate ourselves before you on the ground?" His brothers were jealous of him, but his father kept the matter in mind.* (Genesis 37:10,11)

Yosef meets his Brothers' Wrath

Finally, the brothers could take no more of their anger and decided to kill *Yosef,* their hatred had grown so deep. *Reuven, Ya'akov*'s first son and, therefore the leader of the brothers, ordered *Yosef* not to be killed but to be thrown into a dry cistern. He was obviously a commanding figure, as we read, *But when Re'uven heard this, he saved him from being destroyed by them. He said, "We shouldn't take his life. [22] Don't shed blood,"* Re'uven added. *"Throw him into this cistern here in the wilds, but don't lay hands on him yourselves." He intended to rescue him from them later and restore him to his father.* (Genesis 37:21,22)

Here is where *Adonai Elohim* threw a twist into their plans. At the point they had seized *Yosef* and had thrown him into a nearby dry cistern, a caravan of *Yishma'elim,* Ishmaelites (Descendants of *Yishma'el,* the son of *Avraham* through

> *Yosef's innocence and naivete brought him into conflict with his brothers and prepared the way for his being used by Yahweh.*

Hagar) came by and bought *Yosef* from his brothers. In order to cover their tracks and avoid accountability for their actions, they concocted a really wild story. We find this contained in Genesis 37: *They took Yosef's robe, killed a male goat and dipped the robe in the blood. Then they sent the long-sleeved robe and brought it to their father, saying, "We found this. Do you know if it's your son's robe or not?" He recognized it and cried, "It's my son's robe! Some wild animal has torn Yosef in pieces and eaten him!"* (Genesis 37:31-33) I find it difficult to understand how *Adonai Elohim* could use such evil for His good but, thankfully, I do not have the mind of God.

In the meantime, *Y'hudah* (Judah) moved away from his father's land and started his own family, in the land of Adullam, one of the major Canaanite tribes. The remains of the city may be seen today, overlooking the *Elah* Valley, where the teenage *David* defeated Goliath. Perhaps *Y'hudah* wanted to put some distance between himself and the conspiracy to murder his brother or he wanted to be independent of his father's dominance. We may never know in this life, as Scripture fails to provide a reason. However, this is an important chapter in the story of *Adonai's* people.

Tamar, the Great-Grandmother of *Adonai Yeshua*

The more I read the Hebrew Scriptures, the more fascinated I become of the humanity of our Patriarchs. In Chapter 38, we develop an insight into how sin has grabbed the ancestor of *Adonai Yeshua*. *Y'hudah* essentially took a concubine, *Shua,* 'pit' and through her had three sons. When his firstborn, *Er,* was old enough, *Y'hudah* picked *Tamar,* palm tree, to be his wife; however, *Er* was an evil man and died young, leaving *Tamar* a young widow, without children. The custom of the day called for the closest brother of the deceased husband to take his widow and produce male heirs, to preserve the family line. *Er's* closest brother was *Onan,* strong; to him fell the responsibility of taking Tamar as his wife. *Onan*, realizing any child which would come from their union would not be his, was rebellious and did not follow the tradition of his people. As a result, he too died young.

This left *Tamar* a childless widow, one of the classes of people without protection in the community. *Y'hudah* promised *Tamar* his son *Shelah*, she knows, when he became of age. However, *Y'hudah* forgot his promise and *Tamar*, becoming older, needed to do something or reach the age when she could no longer conceive.

Being a clever person, *Tamar* hatched a plan which would see her bearing a child and, therefore, receiving protection and financial security. Dressing as a prostitute, with a veil to hide her identity, *Tamar* approached *Y'hudah*, who asked to sleep with her. The price for his having sexual relations with her was to be a young goat from his herd. As part of the bargain of payment, *Tamar* demanded *Y'hudah* give her his seal, its cord and the staff he was carrying, until the kid arrived. These were very important items for the leader of a tribe. However, when *Y'hudah* brought the kid to *Tamar*, she was nowhere to be found.

The result of the union of *Y'hudah* and *Tamar* was her pregnancy. When *Tamar* began to show, the tribal members accused her of prostitution, as she was without a husband, and told *Y'hudah*, the tribal leader, of her indiscretion. Following Hebrew tradition at the time, *Y'hudah* ordered *Tamar* to be burned alive, as she had brought dishonour upon the family. As she was brought out to *Y'hudah* and the tribe to receive her punishment, *Tamar* produced the articles she had received from her father-in-law. Upon seeing them, *Y'hudah* realized his sin of breaking his covenant with *Tamar*, asked for her forgiveness and acknowledged her place in the family, as she was now carrying his child.

Why was this chapter included in the Hebrew Scriptures? As I mentioned early into this work, God's instructions for our life come in the form of stories designed to help us understand the direction He desires of us. One of *Adonai*'s instructions focuses on keeping promises.

Y'hudah promised *Tamar* she would marry his son, *Shemar*; however, when his son came of age, he forgot his promise to Tamar. This left Tamar defenceless and vulnerable in a harsh environment. An unclaimed widow received little or no support from families or communities and often had to rely on begging for livelihood. Thus, *Tamar's* plan was designed to force *Y'hudah* to keep his earlier promise to her. Did her plan have the approval of *Adonai*? It worked, didn't it?

> *Adonai Yeshua, the Lord Jesus, came through the union of Tamar and Y'hudah – Yahwehworks in mysterious ways!*

Yosef in Prison

But our story only becomes more intriguing. Returning to the young *Josef*, we find him in Egypt, having been sold to the captain of the Palace Guard, Potiphar. *Yosef* was tasked with looking after his master's house, much like the butler in a modern-day estate. You may read of his duties in Genesis 39. *Yosef* became quite wealthy, as Potiphar's slave. How was this possible? *Adonai* was pleased with *Yosef*; He allowed him to become Potiphar's attendant, bringing him opportunities to gain land and financial gain. However, there was a problem in Potiphar's house – his wife.

Potiphar's wife, unnamed in Scripture, appears to have been a lonely woman, rich and idle without children; there is also the possibility she didn't love her husband. *Yosef* brought excitement and challenge into her life. Several times she invited *Yosef* to her bed but he refused. Read his reasons for refusing in Genesis 39:8,9: *Look, because my master has me, he doesn't know what's going on in this house. He has put all his possessions in my charge. In this house I am his equal; he hasn't withheld anything from me except yourself, because you are his wife. How then could I do such a wicked thing and sin against God!* As her frustration grew so did her scheming. We read of the outcome of her conniving in Genesis 39:11-19 - *However, one day, when he went into the house to do his work, and none of the men living in the house was there indoors, she grabbed him by his robe and said, "Sleep with me!" But he fled, leaving his robe in her hand, and got himself outside. When she saw that he had left his robe in her hand and had escaped, she called the men of her house and said to them, "Look at this! My husband brought in a Hebrew to make fools of us. He came in and wanted to sleep with me, but I yelled out loudly. When he heard me yelling like that, he left his robe with me and ran out." She put the robe aside until his master came home. Then she said to him, "This Hebrew slave you brought us came in to make a fool of me. But when I yelled out, he left his robe with me and fled outside." When his master heard what his wife said as she showed him, "Here's what your slave did to me.* Unfortunately, Potiphar, who obviously loved his wife, believed her story and had *Yosef* thrown into prison. In those days, slaves didn't receive trials when accused of crimes against their masters. Now here is where the story of *Yosef* really becomes interesting.

Adonai's favour continued with *Yosef* while he was in prison. The warden appointed *Yosef* as the prison supervisor, giving him absolute control of the prisoners. Perhaps for the first time, the prison functioned well and prisoners were treated fairly. In any event, *Yosef* prospered, as far as he could in prison. It is estimated *Yosef* stayed in Pharaoh's prison for twelve years, until the age of thirty. A few years after being sentenced, two of pharaoh's attendants, the baker and the chief cupbearer, ran into trouble with pharaoh. Both were sent to prison, where each had a dream. They shared these with *Yosef*; listen to how he approached them, as we read in Genesis 40:8-19, *Yosef said to them, "Don't interpretations belong to God? Tell it to me, please." Then the chief cupbearer told Yosef his dream: "In my dream, there in front of me was a vine, and the vine had three branches. The branches budded, then it suddenly began to blossom, and finally clusters of ripe grapes appeared. Pharaoh's cup was in my hand, so I took the grapes and pressed them into Pharaoh's cup, and gave the cup to Pharaoh." Yosef said to him, "Here is its interpretation: the three branches are three days. Within three days Pharaoh will lift up your head and restore you to your office: you will be giving Pharaoh his cup as you used to when you were his cupbearer. But remember me when it goes well with you; and show me kindness, please; and mention me to Pharaoh, so that he will release me from this prison. For the truth is that I was kidnapped from the land of the Hebrews, and here too I have done nothing wrong that would justify putting me in this dungeon." When the chief baker saw that the interpretation was favorable, he said to Yosef, "I too saw in my dream: there were three baskets of white bread on my head. In the uppermost basket there were all kinds of baked goods for Pharaoh, but the birds ate them out of the basket on my head." Yosef answered, "Here is its interpretation: the three baskets are three days. Within three days Pharaoh will lift up your head from off of you -- he will hang you on a tree, and the birds will eat your flesh off you.*

Parashah 10: Mikketz
(at the end)
Chapters 41:1 to 44:17

Yosef Interprets the Dream;
Yosef becomes Governor

PARASHAH 10: MIKKETZ
(AT THE END)
CHAPTERS 41:1 TO 44:17

Yosef Interprets Pharaoh's Dream

In three days, everything *Yosef* told the cupbearer and the baker came to be; however, the cupbearer forgot his promise to *Yosef* to put a good word forward to pharaoh on his behalf. That is until two years later, when pharaoh himself had two dreams which he could not understand. None of pharaoh's wise men nor his magicians could interpret his dreams; at this point the cupbearer remembered *Yosef* and his ability to interpret even the most obscure dreams. pharaoh ordered *Yosef* released from prison and had him brought before him.

Here are the dreams Pharaoh had, as found in Genesis 41:17-24: *In my dream, I stood at the edge of the river; and there came up out of the river seven cows, fat and sleek; and they began feeding in the swamp grass. After them, there came up out of the river seven more cows, poor, miserable-looking and lean -- I've*

Yosef was released from prison to begin his ministry at the age of 30; Adonai Yeshua was 30 years old, when He was baptized by Yochanan the Immerser

never seen such bad-looking cows in all the land of Egypt! Then the lean and miserable-looking cows ate up the first seven fat cows. But after they had eaten them up, one couldn't tell that they had eaten them; because they were as miserable-looking as before. At this point I woke up. But I dreamed again and saw seven full, ripe ears of grain growing out of a single stalk. After them, seven ears, thin and blasted by the east wind, sprang up. And the thin ears swallowed up the seven ripe ears. I told this to the magicians, but none of them could explain it to me.

Adonai gave Yosef the interpretation of pharaoh's dreams and he relayed them: The dreams of pharaoh are the same: God has told pharaoh what he is about to do. The seven good cows are seven years, and the seven good ears of grain are seven years — the dreams are the same. Likewise the seven lean and miserable-looking cows that came up after them are seven years, and also the seven empty ears blasted by the east wind -- there will be seven years of famine. This is what I told pharaoh: God has shown pharaoh what he is about to do. Here it is: there will be seven years of abundance throughout the whole land of Egypt; but afterwards, there will come seven years of famine; and Egypt will forget all the abundance. The famine will consume the land, and the abundance will not be known in the land because of the famine that will follow, because it will be truly terrible. Why was the dream doubled for pharaoh? Because the matter has been fixed by God, and God will shortly cause it to happen. (Genesis 41:25-32)

Adonai then provided Yosef with the direction pharaoh was to take, in order to secure his people from the devastation of seven years of famine, Therefore, pharaoh should look for a man both discreet and wise to put in charge of the land of Egypt. Pharaoh should do this, and he should appoint supervisors over the land to receive a twenty percent tax on the produce of the land of Egypt during the seven years of abundance. They should gather all the food produced during these good years coming up and set aside grain under the supervision of pharaoh to be used for food *in the cities, and they should store it. This will be the land's food supply for the seven years of famine that will come over the land of Egypt, so that the land will not perish as a result of the famine.* (Genesis 41:33-36)

Pharaoh followed through with *Yosef*'s recommendations and appointed him Governor of Egypt, responsible for the implantation of the famine survival plan.

Here is how this plan was presented to *Yosef*, as we read

Notice Yosef gave all the credit for the dreams' interpretation to Yahweh.

in Genesis 41: *Here, I place you in charge of the whole land of Egypt." Pharaoh took his signet ring off his hand and put it on Yosef's hand, had him clothed in fine linen with a gold chain around his neck and had him ride in his second best chariot; and they cried before him, "Bow down!" Thus he placed him in charge of the whole land of Egypt. Pharaoh said to Yosef, "I, Pharaoh, decree that without your approval no one is to raise his hand or his foot in all the land of Egypt.* (Genesis 41:41-44) In other words, *Yosef* had a free hand to do whatever he needed or wanted to secure Egypt from the impending famine.

In carrying out his plans, *Yosef* also solidified pharaoh's power. Here is how *Torah* describes how he accomplished this: *During the seven years of abundance, the earth brought forth heaps of produce. He collected all the food of these seven years in the land of Egypt and stored it in the cities — the food grown in the fields outside each city he stored in that city. Yosef stored grain in quantities like the sand on the seashore, so much that they stopped counting, because it was beyond measure. . . . The famine was over all the earth, but then Yosef opened all the storehouses and sold food to the Egyptians, since the famine was severe in the land of Egypt. . . . There was no food anywhere, for the famine was very severe, so that both Egypt and Kena'an grew weak* from hunger. Yosef collected all the money there was in Egypt and Kena'an in exchange for the grain they bought, and put the money in Pharaoh's treasury. When all the money in Egypt had been spent, and likewise in Kena'an, all the Egyptians approached Yosef and said, "Give us something to eat, even though we have no money; why should we die before your eyes?" Yosef replied, "Give me your livestock. If you don't have money, I will give you food in exchange for your livestock." So they brought Yosef their livestock; and Yosef gave them food in exchange for the horses, flocks, cattle and donkeys — all that year he provided them with food in exchange for all their livestock. When that year was over, they approached Yosef again and said to him, "We won't hide from my lord that all our money is spent, and the herds of livestock belong to my lord. We have nothing left, as my lord can see, but our bodies and our land. Why should we die before your eyes, both we and our land? Buy us and our land for food, and we and our land will be enslaved to Pharaoh. But also give us seed to plant, so that we can stay alive and not die, and so that the land won't become barren." So Yosef acquired all the land in Egypt for Pharaoh, as one by one the Egyptians sold their fields, because the famine weighed on them so severely. Thus the land became the property of Pharaoh. As for the people, he reduced them to serfdom city by city, from one end of Egypt's territory to the other. [22] Only the priests' land did he not acquire, because the priests were entitled to provisions from Pharaoh, and they ate from what Pharaoh provided them; therefore they did not sell their land. (Genesis 41:47-49; 47:13-22) As Yosef drained all the wealth of Egypt into pharaoh's treasury and built sufficient storehouses for all the grain collected, he also created the most significant infrastructure and governmental oversight Egypt had ever known. This was indeed God in action, as Egypt was never again to see such an organizational structure in its existence, even unto today.

PARASHAH 11: VAYIGASH (HE APPROACHED)
CHAPTERS 44:18 TO 47:27

Yosef Tests his Brothers;
A Second Visit;
Yosef Reveals Himself;
Ya'akov Comes to Egypt;
Ya'akov takes Yosef's Sons as His Own;
Ya'akov Dies

PARASHAH 11: VAYIGASH
(HE APPROACHED)
CHAPTERS 44:18 TO 47:27

Ya'akov's Family comes to Egypt

However, the famine in Egypt is not the only story of note in these final chapters of Genesis. God's plans are perfect and He had a definite plan for the famine which struck the entire Middle East. It appears, while in Cana'an, *Ya'akov* and his sons were also struck by the famine and were forced to seek relief from the wealth of Egypt. *Ya'akov* sent his older sons to purchase food from the vast stores held in the south. And here is where the story really becomes interesting, since they firmly believed their brother, *Yosef*, was a mere slave and had, in all likelihood died in the foreign land.

When they entered Egypt, they were sent to see the Governor, who happened to be their brother. With his Egyptian attire, hair style and make-up, traditional for viziers, they did not recognize their brother and were totally unaware of how *Adonai* was to use *Yosef* in order to humble them and bring them to a state of redemption. Let's examine the events which brought both *Yosef* and his brothers to a state of abject humility.

First, as recorded in Genesis 42, when his brothers faced *Yosef* for the first time in many years, they were treated harshly, even called spies. Why was this done? Before we may reach a state of humility, we must be broken. Brokenness first comes from removing us from our comfort zones and placing us in a state of uncertainty and vulnerability. This is what happened to *Yosef*'s brothers. They were thrown off-guard by *Yosef*'s accusations. Let's read their reactions to these charges, *"No, my lord," they replied, "your servants have come to buy food. We're all the sons of one man, we're upright men; your servants aren't spies. . . . We, your servants, are twelve brothers, the sons of one man in the land of Kena'an; the youngest stayed with our father, and another one is gone."* (Genesis 42:10,11,13) Following their defensive reactions, *Yosef* sets a task before them -- he demands they have their youngest brother, *Binyamin*, Benjamin, be brought to Egypt, to prove they are not lying and has the brothers thrown into prison for three days. Their journey to humility is well under way.

As you will recall, from reading the story of *Yosef*'s being sold to the Midianites (Genesis 37), *Reuben* was the only one who tried to help his brother. Then,  in the presence of the Vizier, he scolds his brothers for their foolish action, the consequences of which they are now facing. *Yosef* understands all they are

> *Before we may reach a state of humility, we must be broken. Brokenness first comes from removing us from our comfort zones and placing us in a state of uncertainty and vulnerability.*

saying and it overwhelms him. He too is being humbled by the unfolding of God's plan.

Nine of the brothers are sent back to *Ya'akov* -- *Simeon* stays behind as 'collateral', to ensure they return with *Binyamin*. Their packs are laden with grain but *Yosef* orders all the money they paid for the grain be secretly placed into their packs. Why did he order this? *Adonai* knew how *Ya'akov* would receive this message. Was it because He wanted a greater degree of pressure on the family to force them back to Egypt? Listen to *Ya'akov's* response, when his sons told him of their adventure: *"You have robbed me of my children! Yosef is gone, Shim'on is gone, now you're taking Binyamin away -- it all falls on me!"* (Genesis 42:36) Once more *Reuben* steps forth and offers assurance for Benjamin's safe return, *"If I don't bring him back to you, you can kill my own two sons! Put him in my care; I will return him to you."* (Genesis 42:37)

Several months later, when the grain they brought from Egypt was nearly exhausted, *Ya'akov's* family once more was forced to return to Egypt, this time with Benjamin in tow. Their entrance into Egypt, this second time, brought a much different reaction from *Yosef.* Rather than placing them in prison, he invited them into his home for a festive meal, the height of Egyptian honour to Israelites, since Egyptians abhorred Israel because of circumcision, which they considered a mutilation of the body. They were taken aback and seemingly frightened, since they left the first time with their grain-filled packs and all their money returned to them. However, *Yosef,* through his interpreter explained to them, *"Stop worrying," he replied, "don't be afraid. Your God and the God of your father put treasure in your packs. As for your money — I was the one who received it." Then he brought Shim'on out to them.* (Genesis 43:23) I don't expect *Simeon* was in prison all this time but was housed in *Yosef's* quarters, as soon as his brothers left. I doubt he had any contact with *Yosef* during this time.

Sitting with his brothers was overwhelming for *Yosef* and he left the room, filled with emotion. Upon his return, he engaged in light conversation with the brothers but heaped Benjamin with an abundance of food and drink, possibly as an expression of his joy.

The next day, as they left with their provisions of grain, *Yosef* ordered his men to place their money into each of his brothers' packs and, in Benjamin's, he was to place *Yosef's* silver goblet. Another step towards humility.

The brothers were accosted by *Yosef's* men, as they were

leaving Egypt. They searched the packs and discovered the goblet, whereupon they seized Benjamin and returned him to *Yosef.* The brothers were undone; hear their remorseful cry, *At this, they tore their clothes from grief. Then each man loaded up his donkey and returned to the city.* (Genesis 44:13) *Y'hudah*, Judah, declared they all were guilty of theft but *Yosef* would not hear of it; he kept Benjamin back and sent the others to *Ya'akov.* Listen to his reasoning: *"Heaven forbid that I should act in such a way. The man in whose possession the goblet was found will be my slave; but as for you, go in peace to your father."* (Genesis 44:17) At this, *Y'hudah* opened his heart to *Yosef* and shared the sins and their consequential troubles, from the plan to kill *Yosef* to the breaking of *Ya'akov*'s heart, if Benjamin was not returned.

Yosef Reveals Himself to His Brothers

This was too much for *Yosef* and, upon clearing the room of everyone but his brothers, proceeded to reveal his true identity to them and relay to them how God used their evil intentions for good. Hear how he revealed *Adonai*'s plans to them: *God sent me ahead of you to ensure that you will have descendants on earth and to save your lives in a great deliverance. So it was not you who sent me here, but God; and he has made me a father to Pharaoh, lord of all his household and ruler over the whole land of Egypt.* (Genesis 45:7,8) *Yosef* then sent them back to their father, with instructions to bring him and his entire household to Egypt. Pharaoh intervened and gave to them the land of *Goshen*, the fertile delta of the Nile River, as their new home.

In Genesis 46, *Moses*, who scribed *Torah*, has included the names of all the families arriving in *Goshen*, as a way of showing the importance of this relocation and fulfillment of one more step in God's plans for redemption.

The relationship between *Yosef* and *Ya'akov*, while in Egypt, was quite strained. On *Yosef*'s part, he did not go to his father's side, in Goshen, but sent his wife, Aseneth, to care for him. *Yosef* was afraid his presence before *Ya'akov* would result in *Ya'akov's* questioning him regarding the circumstances of his coming to Egypt; this would

The moment Ya'acov and his family (74, including Yosef, his 2 sons and his wife, Aseneth) settled in Egypt, this began the 450 years of Israel's exile in this foreign land.

have brought shame upon his brothers and also *Ya'akov*. This shame might have impelled *Ya'akov* to curse *Yosef's* sons, thus condemning them to death. There were other concerns *Yosef* had: *a.* would *Ya'akov* bless *Ephraim*, fruitful. and Manasseh, causing to forget, who were Egyptians; *b.* if he did would he place them in positions of power by appointing them head of tribes; *c.* would *Ya'akov* assign the rights of the first born to him, as he was his father's favourite in Cana'an; *d.* in doing so, would he remove the rights of the first born from *Reuven*, who was the legitimate first born son and *e.* why had *Ya'akov* buried *Rachel*, *Yosef's* mother, along the roadside, instead of the family plot at *Machpelah*? However, *Yosef* wanted to be informed of his father's health constantly, so he had a messenger travel between *Goshen* and *Yosef's* home along the Nile River.

On his part, *Ya'akov* was concerned about the possibility of his family assimilating into Egyptian culture, where he would die and be buried (he wanted to be buried with his father, *Avraham*, and his first wife, *Leah*). Also, he wanted to be able to see *Yosef* and his children. As we read, in Genesis 46, *Adonai Elohim* spoke with *Ya'akov* in a dream and assured him, *I am God, the God of your father. Don't be afraid to go down to Egypt. It is there that I will make you into a great nation. Not only will I go down with you to Egypt; but I will also bring you back here again, after Yosef has closed your eyes.* (Genesis 46:3,4) With this assurance, *Ya'akov* freely travelled to Egypt.

Just before his death, *Ya'akov* had an occasion to bless *Yosef*'s two sons, *Ephraim* and *Manasseh*. The names of *Yosef*'s sons are highly significant: *Ephraim* means 'fruitfulness', whereas *Manasseh* means 'forgetfulness'. For whatever reason, perhaps because *Yosef* had become more Egyptian in his way of life, *Ya'akov* took *Yosef*'s sons, *Ephraim* and *Manasseh* as his own. This would give *Ya'akov* the right to bless these young boys as his own. However, rather than giving the blessing of the first born to *Manasseh*, he crossed his arms and placed his right hand on *Ephraim*'s head, indicating *Ephraim* was to be the stronger and spiritually attentive son. From *Ephraim* would emerge the tribe of *Ephraim*, one of the ten northern tribes of Israel, lost in the Assyrian exile and diaspora into the Assyrian Empire. I find it interesting the number of peoples living around the world today who claim to be descendants of Ephraim, such as many within the British Commonwealth, especially the British themselves.

From *Manasseh* emerged *Gideon*, the judge from the Book of Judges, who led the Israelites against the Midianites.

Ya'akov died shortly after blessings *Yosef*'s two sons. He had instructed *Yosef* to have his body buried in Cana'an. However, as *Yosef* was very much in the culture of Egypt, rather than following the traditional Israelite customs of burial. *Yosef* had his father's body embalmed. *Ya'akov*'s now embalmed corpse was in view for seventy days, following the 40-day embalming ritual. Only then did *Yosef* carry out his father's wishes and had *Ya'akov*'s body carried the Cana'an and buried in the caves of *Machpelah*, with *Avraham* and *Sarah*.

> *Is there evidence to suggest there are millions of descendants of the ten lost tribes of Israel now living throughout the world? DNA evidence suggests there are.*

PARASHAH 12: VAYECHI (HE LIVED)
CHAPTERS 47:28 TO 50:26

Ya'akov Blesses His Sons; Yosef and His Brothers Reconciled

PARASHAH 12: VAYECHI
(HE LIVED)
CHAPTERS 47:28 TO 50:26

Ya'akov Blesses His Sons

Shortly before his death, as recorded in Genesis 49, *Ya'akov* blessed each of his sons. Some of these might be called mixed blessings, at the very least; however, each also contained a prophecy of things to come. Specifically, *Ya'akov* shared his blessings within the context of the perilous times, which many theologians claim refers to the end-times.

The blessings for *Reuven*, the first born, were not positive. Listen to the words *Ya'akov* used to describe his perception of his oldest son: *Re'uven, you are my firstborn, my strength, the firstfruits of my manhood. Though superior in vigor and power you are unstable as water, so your superiority will end.* (Genesis 49:3,4) Why did *Ya'akov* have such a negative perspective of his first born -- because *Reuven* violated his father's bed, by sleeping with his concubine; this was one of the most heinous acts a child might commit against his father.

Ya'akov perceived *Shim'on* and *Levi* as violent and angry, destroying property and reputations, rather than building. Remember, as we read in Genesis 34, *Shim'on* and *Levi* destroyed the city of *Shekhem* and killed all its males, when their sister, *Dinah*, was violated by *Shekhem*, the son of the ruler of the city. *Ya'akov* never forgot that act and felt it was a stain on his name and that of his family. Thus, his 'blessing' was a mixed one, to say the least. Listen to the words he uses, *Let me not enter their council, let my honor not be connected with their people.* (Genesis 49:6) Their fate, then, was to be scattered amongst other tribes, separated from each other, so they could not feed each other's anger, as they had done in *Shekhem. Shim'on* was to be mixed with *Y'hudah,* while *Levi* did not receive an inheritance of his own but was to be served by all the tribes. *Levi* became to tribe of Temple workers, scattered throughout the other tribes. We read of this in Volume Two: *Shemot*/Exodus

Y'hudah, although not the eldest son, received the blessing usually reserved for the eldest son. His would be the strength of Israel, keeping the nation strong and guarded. Indeed, King *David* emerged from the tribe of *Y'hudah* and, more importantly, *Adonai Yeshua,* the Lord Jesus, was born to *Myriam,* who descended from *David.* This may have been the meaning of *Ya'akov's* cryptic blessing, *The scepter will not pass from Y'hudah.* (Genesis 49:10) Through his blessing to *Y'hudah* (meaning 'praise you, Lord'), *Ya'akov* obviously was given vision into the distant future, for the following references are clearly related to Messiah *Yeshua* - *Tying his donkey to the vine, his donkey's colt to the choice grapevine, he washes his clothes in wine, his robes in the blood of grapes.* (Genesis 49:11) The grapevine is a symbol of sustenance and refreshment, provided by *Adonai* Himself to His people. The donkey was the animal ridden by kings, when they came to a foreign land; riding the donkey was a symbol of peace, while riding a horse was the symbol for riding off to war.

Ya'akov's blessing to his son, *Z'vulun* – the sixth son of *Ya'akov,* carries with it the promise of prosperity, as signified by the phrase, *Z'vulun will live at the seashore, with ships anchoring along his coast and his border at Tzidon.* (Genesis 49:13) His name in Hebrew means dwelling or habitation. At this time in Middle Eastern history, they will be a conduit for trade, allowing ships to bring and receive cargo. They will also become a transit point for *Torah* to be taken around the known world.

Yissakhar was *Ya'akov's* ninth son; his name means reward. He was to head a tribe which would toil mightily (*he will bend his back to the burden and submit to forced labor*) but will reap prosperity from his labours (*On seeing how good is settled life and how pleasant the country*). Not only was this a prophecy of the time of slavery in Egypt, it was focused on what would happen to this tribe, when they settled in the Promised Land.

The word *Dan*, in Hebrew, means judgment. Dan was *Ya'akov's* fifth son and his tribe indeed become *a viper on the road*; the tribe of *Dan* was given territory along the land controlled by the Philistines. Having been harassed by the Philistines for centuries and, finally believing they were too weak to overcome, even with *Yahweh's* strength, the people of the tribe moved north and forcefully took land from the weaker tribe of *Manasseh.*

Gad was the seventh son on *Ya'akov*, by his concubine, *Zilpah*, the handmaid of *Leah*, *Ya'akov's* first wife. The short blessing given to Gad contains a cryptic meaning: *Gad [troop] -- a troop will troop on him, but he will troop on their heel.* Here we read a prophetic word from God to *Ya'akov* about the tribe of *Gad.* They were fierce warriors for King *David*, as we read in 1 Chronicles 12:14,15 - *These descendants of Gad were army commanders; the least of them was worth a hundred, and the greatest worth a thousand. These are the men who crossed the Yarden during the first month, when it had overflowed all its banks, and drove out all those who lived in the valleys, both to the east and to the west.* The prophesy continues, as in Jeremiah 49:1 - *Then why has Malkam inherited Gad, with his people settled in its cities? Malkam*, God is their Ruler, in this passage, refers to the Assyrian commander who, in 1891 BCE, came upon the northern tribe of *Gad* and took many of the people of *Gad* back to Assyria as captives.

Ya'akov's blessing of *Asher* informs us of the abundance

Adonai Elohim placed within this faithful tribe. Listen to the words uttered by *Ya'akov*: *Asher's food is rich -- he will provide food fit for a king.* (Genesis 49:20). The tribe of *Asher* will be the source of abundance of the kind of food people within the region needed to not only survive but thrive. In addition, by saying the tribe will provide food fit for a king, *Ya'akov* was prophesizing the provision of not only necessities but luxuries as well.

Naftali received what may only be characterized as a messianic prophecy. Read the blessing from *Ya'akov* carefully: *Naftali is a doe set free that bears beautiful fawns.* (Genesis 49:21) The first part of the blessings, *Naftali is a doe set free*, refers to the territory this tribe occupied. Here, situated at the northern edge of Lake Kinneret, perhaps better known as the Sea of Galilee, is the region known as the Galilee, where many of the Samarians lived. *Naftali* was the region in which *Adonai Yeshua*, the Lord Jesus, spent most of His time preaching, healing and creating signs and wonders. Quoting from Isaiah 8:23 to 9:1, *Adonai Yeshua* claims the people in this region have been saved from eternal death through accepting His as the Light of the world, *Land of Z'vulun and land of Naftali, toward the lake, beyond the Yarden, Galil-of-the-Goyim -- the people living in darkness have seen a great light; upon those living in the region, in the shadow of death, light has dawned.* (Matthew 4:15,16)

The blessings *Yosef* received from *Ya'akov* are both complex and rich. Let's read it in its entirety: *Yosef is a fruitful plant, a fruitful plant by a spring, with branches climbing over the wall. The archers attacked him fiercely, shooting at him and pressing him hard; but his bow remained taut; and his arms were made nimble by the hands of the Mighty One of Ya'akov, from there, from the Shepherd, the Stone of Isra'el, by the God of your father, who will help you, by El Shaddai, who will bless you with blessings from heaven above, blessings from the deep, lying below, blessings from the breasts and the womb. The blessings of your father are more powerful than the blessings of my parents, extending to the farthest of the everlasting hills; they will be on the head of Yosef, on the brow of the prince among his brothers.* (Genesis 49:22-26) We need to examine this one section at a time.

Yosef is a fruitful plant, a fruitful plant by a spring, with branches climbing over the wall. Calling *Yosef* a fruitful plant, with branches climbing over the wall, *Ya'akov* is referring to the fruitfulness of the sons of *Yosef*, *Ephraim* and *Manasseh*, who received their blessings earlier (see Genesis 48).

The archers attacked him fiercely, shooting at him and pressing him hard; but his bow remained taut; and his arms were made nimble by the hands of the Mighty One of Ya'akov – Here we see a beautiful picture of *Yahweh's* hands upon *Yosef's* descendants, strengthening him when attacked, even when they were unaware of His strengthening them.

from the Shepherd, the Stone of Isra'el, by the God of your father, who will help you, by El Shaddai, who will bless you with blessings from heaven above, blessings from the deep, lying below, blessings from the breasts and the womb. In effect, *Yosef,* through *Ephraim* and *Manasseh,* received the double portion of the firstborn son. This portion of the blessing indicates *Yosef's* growth as a populous tribe, becoming the largest tribes of the twelve.

The blessings of your father are more powerful than the blessings of my parents, extending to the farthest of the everlasting hills. As we have discovered, *Ya'akov* lived most of his life as a scoundrel, hardly a faithful, obedient son. When he realized the error of his ways and repented, *Yahweh* forgave him of the sins committed and brought him salvation. Thus, the blessing *Ya'akov* placed upon *Yosef* was timeless and more powerful than the blessings extended to *Ya'akov*. I find it interesting to read of the titles *Ya'akov* has given *Yahweh* in this blessing: *Shepherd, Stone of Isra'el, God of your father, El Shaddai.* This is quite different from an earlier understanding of *Yahweh*, when *Ya'akov* referred to Him as the God of *Abraham* and Fear of His Father *Isaac*. By using these four labels, *Ya'akov* recognizes *Yahweh* is his *Elohim*, his God.

The final blessing was given to *Ya'akov's* youngest son, *Binyamin,* Son of the Right Hand: *Binyamin is a ravenous wolf, in the morning devouring the prey, in the evening still dividing the spoil.* (Genesis 49:27) History records *Binyamin* as one of the fiercest of the twelve tribes; indeed, in Judges 19 and 20, we are told of the atrocities committed by the men of Binyamin. Interestingly, *Rav Sha'ul,* the Apostle Paul, was from the tribe of *Binyamin* and we know of his ferocious passion, first against believers in *Adonai Yeshua* and then, after his eyes were opened on the road to Damascus (Acts 19), his attempts to convert pagans to Messianic worship.

Yosef and His Brothers are Reconciled

Ya'akov's final words to his sons charged them with burying his body with *Avraham, Sarah* and *Yitzchak* in the caves of *Makhpelah,* the land *Avraham* bought from the sons of *Het.* Our first book of *Torah* finishes with the complete restoration of *Yosef* with his brothers; this is a most poignant moment – here we see true repentance and forgiveness. Let's review this moment: *Realizing that their father was dead, Yosef's brothers said, "Yosef may hate us now and pay us back in full for all the suffering we caused him."* [16] *So they sent a message to Yosef which said, "Your father gave this order before he died:* [17] *'Say to Yosef, "I beg you now, please forgive your brothers' crime and wickedness in doing you harm."' So now, we beg of you, forgive the crime of the servants of the God of your father." Yosef wept when they spoke to him;* [18] *and his brothers too came, prostrated themselves before him and said, "Here, we are your slaves."* [19] *But Yosef said to them, "Don't be afraid! Am I in the place of God?* [20] *You meant to do me harm, but God meant it for good — so that it would come about as it is today, with many people's lives being saved. So don't be afraid — I will provide for you and your little ones." In this way he comforted them, speaking kindly to them.* (Genesis 50:15-21) I personally find the interchange, initiated by *Yosef's* brothers, to be intriguing. Notice they first admit their guilt, for having sold *Yosef* to the Midianites, and committed themselves to him, in reparation for the damages their actions caused. *Yosef*'s response was characterized as graceful and kind, indicating the presence of the Hand of Yahweh throughout the years. To me, this signifies the grace extended to everyone who turns back to *HaShem*, the God of Israel and authentically asks for forgiveness of sins committed and pledges to serve only Him.

Here, then, we finish the Book of Genesis – *B'resheit* – In the Beginning.

CHAZAK! CHAZAK! VENISCHAZIK!
BE STRONG! BE STRONG! AND MAY WE BE STRENGTHENED!

CONCLUSION

As you are now reading the final page of A Journey Through Torah, we hope your knowledge and understanding of Yahweh's Life Instructions to His children have increased. We would very much enjoy hearing from you, your comments and your questions. If you have a recommendation for improving this first volume, we would be delighted to hear from you. Every comment or question will be personally addressed by either Michael or Glenn. You may contact us, through the following e-mail: heartformessiah@gmail.com

Volume 2 of this series - *Sh'mot*, Exodus, will be forthcoming. We hope and pray each volume will add to your spiritual growth and understanding of God's call upon your lives.

May the God of Abraham, Isaac and Jacob bless you richly.

Michael Wodlinger   Glenn Sikorski

MAPS OF GENESIS

LOCATION OF THE TOWER OF BABEL

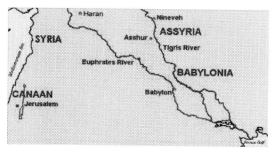

Possible location of the Tower of Babel, between the Tigris and Euphrates Rivers
Genesis 11
(Used with Permission from Bible Hub)

Abram's Journey from Ur

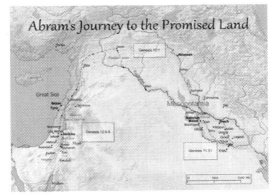

Genesis 12
(Used with Permission from Bible Hub)

SODOM AND GOMORRAH

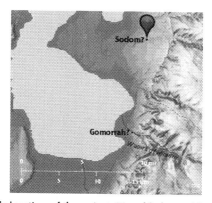

Possible Locations of the ancient cities of Sodom and Gomorrah
by the Dead Sea
Genesis 19
(Used with Permission from Bible Hub)

ABRAM RESCUES LOT

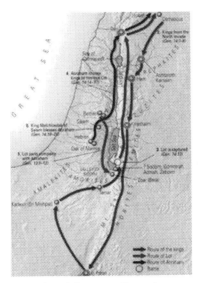

Abram's Journey to Rescue Lot
Genesis 14
Used with permission from e-BibleTeacher.com

ABRAHAM SACRIFICES ISAAC

The Location of Mount Moriah

The Temple of Solomon was built on Mt. Moriah, where
Abraham offered Isaac as a sacrifice to Yahweh
Genesis 22
(Used with Permission from Bible Hub)

ELIEZER'S JOURNEY TO FIND A WIFE FOR ISAAC

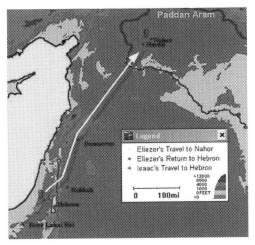

Genesis 24
Used with permission from e-BibleTeacher.com

Ya'akov's Journeys

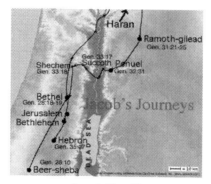

Genesis 28 to 32
(Used with Permission from Bible Hub)

YOSEF'S JOURNEY TO EGYPT

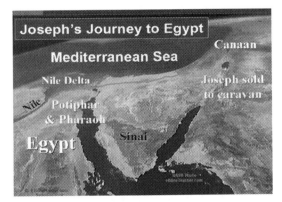

Genesis 37
Used with permission from e-BibleTeacher.com
Satellite Photo from NASA

Ya'akov's Journey to Goshen

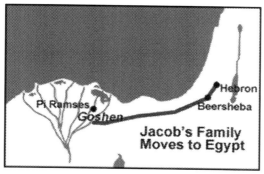

Genesis 46
Used with permission from e-BibleTeacher.com

ABOUT THE AUTHOR
AND ILLUSTRATOR

Michael Wodlinger:

Michael Wodlinger is a Jewish believer who was raised in a Jewish home in Toronto. His grandparents immigrated to Canada from the Ukraine in the late 1800s.

Michael Wodlinger has been a professional educator for over 50 years, as teacher, administrator, researcher, author, consultant and counsellor. He has a Master of Theological Study in Spiritual Formation at Tyndale Seminary, Toronto, a Master's degree from the University of Toronto, in Educational Theory and a Doctorate from the University of Alberta, focusing on educational administration.

Michael has been working with educators in industry, health services, education, and churches. Prior to his retirement, Michael was employed as Associate Professor of Education and Director of University Research at Nipissing University, Ontario and, most recently, an adjunct professor with Tindale Seminary, Toronto, Ontario, Canada. An author of several books on adult education, reflective practice, effective mentoring and numerous other publications, Michael has focused his professional activities on critical thinking, decision making and mentoring skills.

Michael came to faith in Messiah Jesus later in life. Intrigued by the changes in his wife, Chantal, when she first came to faith, Michael's curiosity and the gentle ministry of dear friends eventually brought him to the Lord. A Chosen People Ministries staff member had the privilege of praying with him when Michael decided to trust in the Lord.

Michael began his latest phase of career and ministry by serving with Chosen People Ministries in Toronto, Winnipeg and most recently Quebec where Michael and Chantal create and broadcast monthly Bible Studies and weekly Devotions through their website: www.heartformessiah.org, You Tube and Facebook. Michael and Chantal are active in the community, volunteering and sharing the Gospel. Michael and Chantal are currently discipling a small group of adult Believers and their children who are discovering their Hebraic roots.

Glenn Sikorski:

In the year 1985, someone planted the seeds of Biblical thought in my mind. I became a follower then at age 28. In recent times, like my friend Michael Wodlinger, I have found that the historical background of scriptures has enriched my perspective very much.

Cartooning became a fascination to me in 1982. I have had many cartoons published in newspapers and greeting cards. Illustrating this book has been a pleasure.

Printed in the United States
By Bookmasters